FROM THE BOOKS OF
Lou and Nancy Schloss

New Adventures in
NEEDLEPOINT DESIGN

by Natalie Hays Hammond

SIMON AND SCHUSTER · NEW YORK

ACKNOWLEDGMENTS

As gratitude and happiness are twin emotions, I am delighted for this opportunity to thank my friends for their help in the preparation of this book. I am indebted to Marianne Huebner for her expert professional advice; to Grace Schaefer for hours of work cataloguing and filing my over seven hundred needlepoint designs; to Cora Anthony and the kind people who sent me source material; and to Phyllis Connard, who bought my first needlepoint in my Boston exhibition.

I also thank Clarence F. Korker, of the Ridgefield Photo Shop, for his patient and meticulous work in preparing the black-and-white photographs for this book.

SBN 671-21575-2
Library of Congress Catalog Card Number: 73–10927
Designed by Eve Metz
Manufactured in the United States of America

1 2 3 4 5 6 7 8 9 10

To
ELIZABETH H. TAYLOR
with
affectionate gratitude

CONTENTS

Introduction

It is meet and proper that one not versed in the technique of the craft should introduce a book on needlepoint. One acquainted with the intricacies could hardly do more than evaluate or elaborate or ingeminate. But a lay witness can approach an art with a sense of wonder and astonishment, and he can record an enjoyment that comes from response rather than savvy. Further, the lay brother is likely to detect details and catch secular asides that give art a human setting and put it on the plane of the daily, relating it to other than purely aesthetic activities.

My acquaintance over the years with the rich and varied life and work of Natalie Hays Hammond gives me an appreciation of her needlepoint that I should not have if I knew only the content of this book and what it bespeaks. The author conceals more talent than many an artist reveals. She hides her light under a bushel of abilities. Many of her effects, and almost all of her philosophy, derive from a translation of other art forms into needlepoint.

Thus the items on the pages that follow are but a brilliant spin-off of a ball of fire. The canvases done to date by the artist number almost a thousand, and yet they are but an integrated fragment of what she has lavishly produced in other fields of creative endeavor. The genius all of us can appreciate lies in the fact that Miss Hammond has expressed her ideas in many forms of art, and, as *The Boston Herald* points out, in all of them she has been successful and in many outstanding: "Whatever her medium may be, she knows it thoroughly. Her use of color is incisive and clear, her watercolors have charm without vagueness, her crayons are whimsically styled, and in her pencil drawings is a melancholy strength."

Beyond the media mentioned she has shown skill and percipience in the design of theater sets. In her costume work, *Art News* says, she is brief, smart, and knowing. Her work also and in particular includes the exacting and precise art of the miniature, in which she has had extraordinary success. Soon after taking up the development of this form she became the youngest exhibitor in a display put on at the Royal Academy in London and shortly thereafter was elected the youngest associate in the history of The Royal Miniature Society of Painters, Sculptors and Gravers.

Because of the scope of her interests and the amplitude of her abilities, the author of *New Adventures in Needlepoint Design* may well be regarded as an environment rather than an artist. She provides ambiance. Her mind surrounds and cultivates what is good. And as if to make this point and the fact of it concrete, she founded in 1958 the Hammond Museum and Research Center at North Salem, New York. She assembled a fraction of what she had accumulated in the pursuit of the arts and saw it housed in a building of rare beauty fittingly called The Guild Hall. Hard by The Guild Hall she caused to be laid out and constructed a remarkable pleasance known as The Stroll Garden, wispy and delicate in motif. The paradigm and the pleached paths of it are no less a revelation of Miss Hammond's sense of design than are some of her formal works on paper.

During the years the Museum has been open to the public and has enjoyed the support of an increasing membership, it has helped to fulfill one of the noblest purposes of art: to create an ever-present awareness of beauty and to bind people together with hoops of common concern. A succession of carefully planned and assembled exhibits has kept the purpose alive and growing. There have been integrated circuits dealing with the religions of the world, the theater, picturesque history as shown in heraldry, commerce as a means of communication—and there is one coming up on the Orient.

It was on a chance (perhaps I should say providential) visit to the Hammond Museum that I met the director and found that we shared an interest in the mystery and history of London. From my own close study I felt competent to judge what she had assembled and, above all, what she had written about the shards she had put in pattern. Her captions showed patient and shrewd research and her findings were sound and verifiable. At the same time she had found ways of putting her stuff with freshness and verve. I admired the captions or legends, and those I saw at later exhibits, because they demonstrated not only an ability to select telling scenes but also a rare power to interpret, to talk to me about art. The person who wrote them, I said to myself, has perspicuity as great as her perspicacity.

At the Museum and in the most favorable circumstances, then, I saw the display of needlepoint from which most of the pictures in the present book were chosen. There were 348 pieces, ranging in size from 7 x 11 inches to a large panel measuring 53¼ x 34¼ inches. Many more have been made since by the unceasing creative fingers of the artist, and from these some further selections have been made.

I had the advantage of seeing the pieces in what might be called their natural habitat, their beauty cast against the background of grace provided by the artist. And, as always at the Hammond, the captions and guidelines were witty and to the point, as in the case of the two geese flying in slightly confused formation, one bird saying to the other, "We turn right at the Sunoco station."

On the whole, there was a gaiety about the show, as there is in whatever Natalie Hays Hammond does, even though it may be hidden behind decorum. Small wonder that the canvases at the Hammond attracted viewers from the region roundabout and, as it lasted and the word spread, appealed especially to men for its color and freedom and imagination and the appearance of ease with which the work had been done. The success of the show and the beauty of the work aroused the interest of an alert publisher sensitive to expanding tastes and led to this book.

It is a pity that but a fraction of the thousands who buy the book will have had the experience of seeing the show that prompted it. But there are compensations aplenty. There is value in having precise instructions that can lead to a do-it-alone approach. There is also value in understanding the philosophy and grasping those theories and ideas that can be of use to all of us in any kind of creative work we undertake.

There is, to begin with, the encouragement of courage given by the artist. If the work to be done and the purpose sought in this book had to be stated quickly, it would be, surely, to make the reader bold. Miss Hammond liberates the mind of the reader from the trappings of convention in the selection of subject matter. You are to make your own choice of what you want to represent, aided by suggestions drawn from the author's experience. Many of these are embraced in the well-executed drawings of her superb *Anthology of Pattern* (New York, 1949). Other suggestions are offered in such categories as hobo and electronic signs. Everything is up-to-date in the Hammond approach. The world of symbol is her parish, and she will allow none to force the nascent artist toward cutouts and pasteups.

There is further encouragement given to freedom and elbow room in the very nature of the stitch the author uses and advocates. Her work is done in gros point, a method that calls for what is known in common parlance as the continental or tent stitch. The stiches are large, and each crosses two vertical and two horizontal threads in the mesh of the canvas. Gros point releases the inhibitions of the fingers and gives them a sense of the minute in handling the infinite.

Still another aspect of Miss Hammond's work can hearten the neophyte. This is her directness. She does not parry with preliminaries or squander time on sketches. What impressed Joseph T. Butler, American editor of *The Connoisseur*, in reviewing the needlepoint show was that each of the panels in the display at the Museum "had been conceived in Miss Hammond's mind and executed directly on the canvas. In no case had the design been drawn and then filled out. This direct communication with the canvas gives a vitality to the pictures which could be achieved in no other manner."

It also gives a vitality to the person who plies the needle, to the student or understudy who cannot hope to achieve results comparable to those that attend the work of Natalie Hays Hammond but does hope that he can achieve some measure of her satisfaction. Her book will be a guide to confident endeavor, and when she tells you to think needlepoint, you'll find that for a long time to come you'll remain under her influence, and it will not be easy or possible to think anything else.

—CHARLES W. FERGUSON

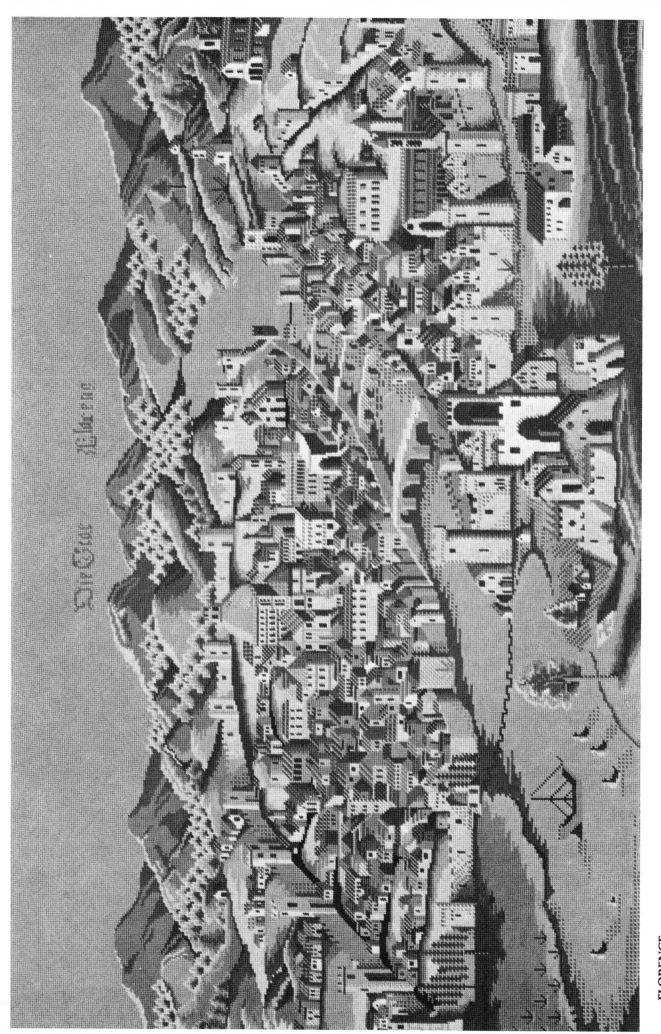

FLORENCE

Needlepoint executed from a wood-block illustration in Sebastian Münster's *Cosmographia universalis* or *Beschreibung aller Länder*, the first detailed, scientific and popular description of the world, in German, according to the Britannica. Münster (1489–1552) was a geographer, mathematician and Hebraist and was the first German to edit the Hebrew Bible, 1534–1535.

Foreword

Were I to say that my interest in needlework never extended beyond the uninspired little classes of school sewing that girls used to be subjected to, and that I literally "fell" into needlepoint in mid-career, it would be close to fact. For it so happened that I betrayed my astrological sign, Capricorn (the cautious and surefooted goat of the zodiac), by hurtling from a twenty-foot construction wall onto a heap of jagged paving stones, injuring my back, but of course saving my brand-new wristwatch. The foolish accident necessitated a number of operations and interminable hospital incarcerations in the following four years.

I was a painter-designer, working long hours at drawing board and easel. Naturally the doctors stopped such activities, and I was forced to find a portable craft that could be managed in bed.

A childhood memory solved the problem. I recalled my mother and aunt and an elderly neighbor on the terrace of our summer home doing needlepoint. The scene was peaceful—the three women seated in wicker armchairs, chintz bags of yarn by their sides, bright-colored dresses dappled by sunlight slanting through the tall oak branches. The sound of cozy conversation and occasional laughter surrounded them like a moat of contentment.

That flashback started me on the enchanting but confusing path of needlepoint. Enchanting because of the palette of wools and silks and the opportunity for design experiment. Confusing because of my complete ignorance of stitchery. Rejecting the idea of filling in backgrounds of stamped designs, I looked for graphic material that could be transposed to canvas. Among my most treasured possessions were a number of sixteenth-century wood-engraved city maps from the *Cosmographia Universalis*. They were loose pages from a book approximately ten by twelve inches in size. To preserve the detail, the scale obviously had to be enlarged, especially as I had decided on the simplest basic stitch, gros point, for my first endeavor. Drawn on the canvas they became five-foot panels!

I was a fool who rushed in happily where an experienced needlewoman would have paled at the thought of working without a frame, let alone tackling so intricate a pattern on a first attempt. But looking at the charming narrow streets, the graceful church spires, the crowded covered bridges of Florence, as Muenster depicted them in 1549, I started my adventure into the new medium by working the muted blues of the winding Arno, picturesquely dotted with oversized ducks.

As I worked each building I lived in it in

imagination, hearing the cacophony of the busy thoroughfares, the turmoil of marketplaces, and feeling the pale spring sunlight on the river's edge. The project offered not only technical challenge but a most absorbing journey back through time.

The problems of stylizing tiled roofs, cobbled squares, and meadows and woodlands made me forget the irksome routine of the hospital. In fact, when a young intern dropped into my room one day to inquire about my physical condition, I answered absentmindedly, "Fine, except for the trees." Seeing his amazement, I hastily explained that the diminishing perspective of a needlepoint forest was far more harassing than the discomfort of an injured back.

The first panel was finished in three months, and I immediately started a second medieval city from the *Cosmographia*. It was the fortified German town of Rufach, high in the Alps. The crenellated battlements towered above mountain streams and scattered farms. In imagination I could hear the whisper of winter snows in evergreen branches and see the fine filigree of frost on windowpanes of the half-timbered houses. With confidence bolstering enthusiasm, the five-foot panel was finished in ten weeks.

The fact that cities—old or new—mirror the aspirations, activities, or despair of their inhabitants led me to study the commerce and trade of the two I had worked in needlepoint. This was the beginning of an absorbing interest—symbolism.

Symbols I have always thought of as the footnotes of history, their messages specific and brief. The symbols of pictographic languages, of trademarks, merchants' marks, house marks, possession marks, are often incredibly modern in feeling. But then, from the point of design, the old is as new as the shortness of memory. Some of these symbols may reveal the transition from mythical symbolism to religious. Some commemorate the founding of a guild, while other signs recall the skills, the patient lifetimes of work of nameless artisans.

Mainly on this theme I have worked some six hundred needlepoint designs in the last six years, without even scratching the surface of the source material. Predominantly they have been ancient Egyptian, Persian, Chinese, Hebrew, Byzantine, Greek, and early medieval designs, though I have not overlooked the great wealth of symbolism inherent in our modern technologies.

At this point a needlewoman would give detailed and effective advice on workmanship. I must admit that I have executed all my needlepoint in gros point on #10 penelope canvas, for my primary concern has been with the designs appropriate to the medium. I have looked enviously at the crewelwork and other lovely stitchery and embroidery produced by friends. But I am a Capricorn, and have followed the single track.

—NATALIE HAYS HAMMOND

North Salem, New York
1973

14

Part One

THINK
IN NEEDLEPOINT

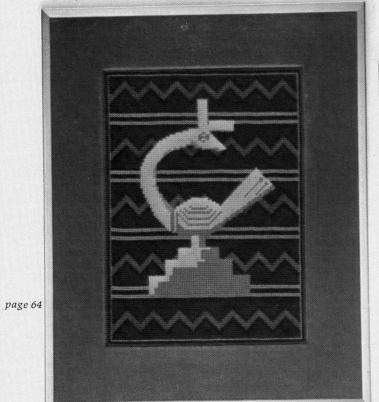

page 64

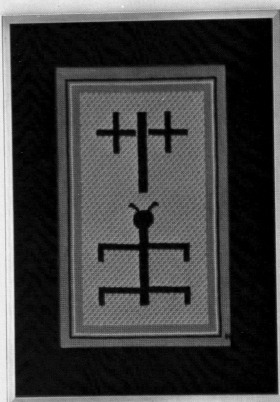

page 56

page 106

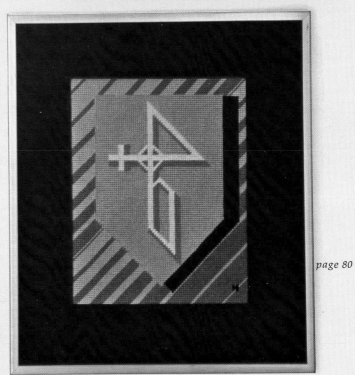

page 80

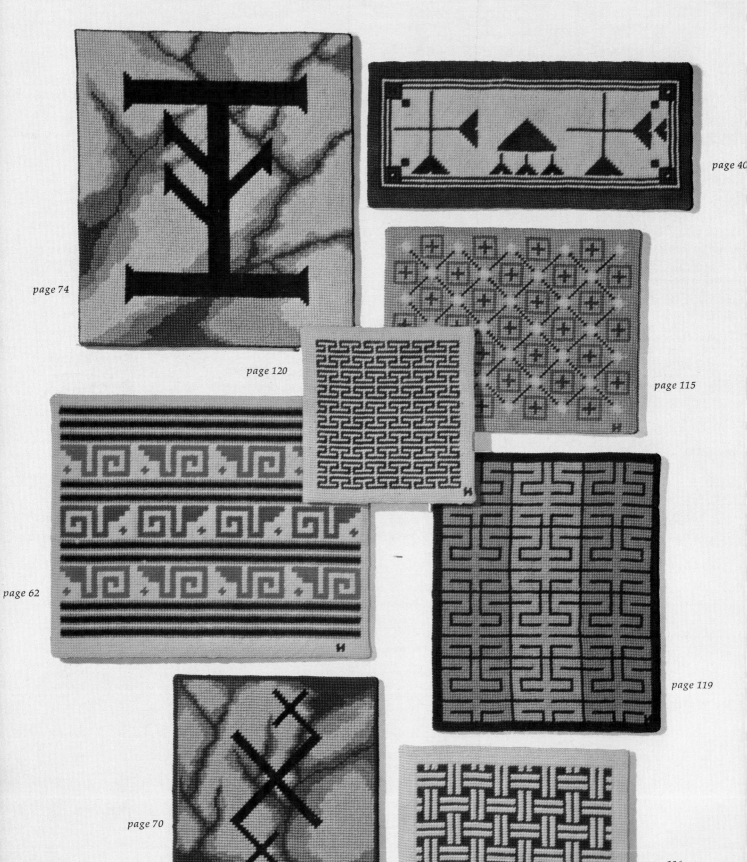

page 74

page 40

page 115

page 120

page 62

page 119

page 70

page 116

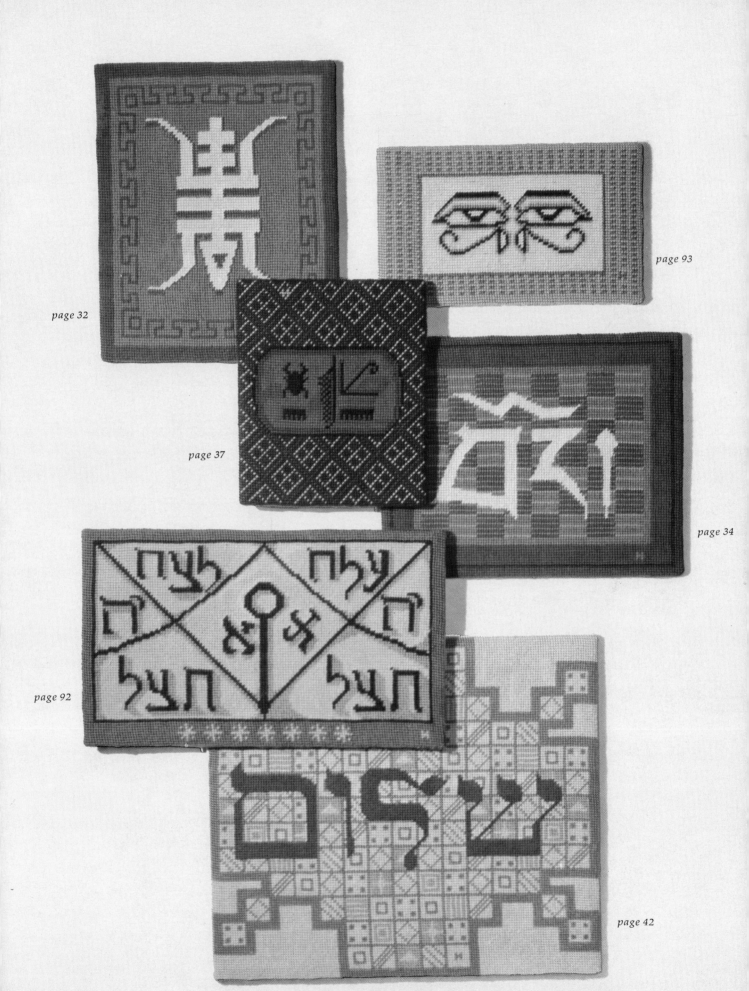

page 32

page 93

page 37

page 34

page 92

page 42

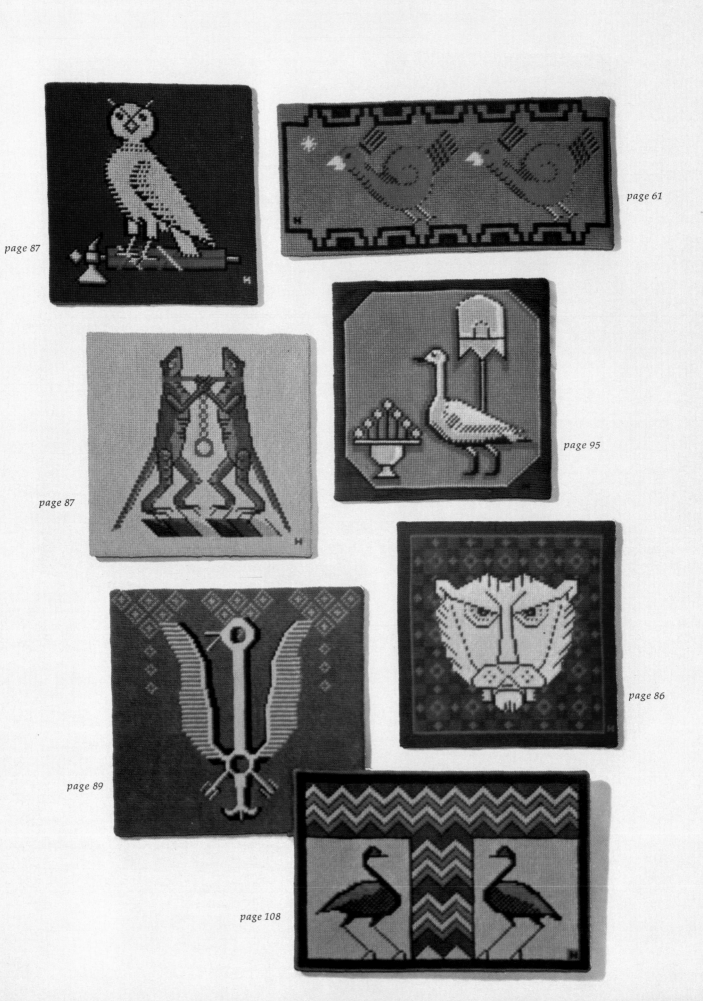

page 87

page 61

page 87

page 95

page 89

page 86

page 108

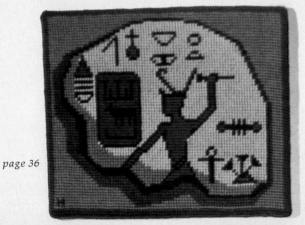

page 36

page 94

page 39

page 27

page 90

TESTVDINE

page 33

page 96

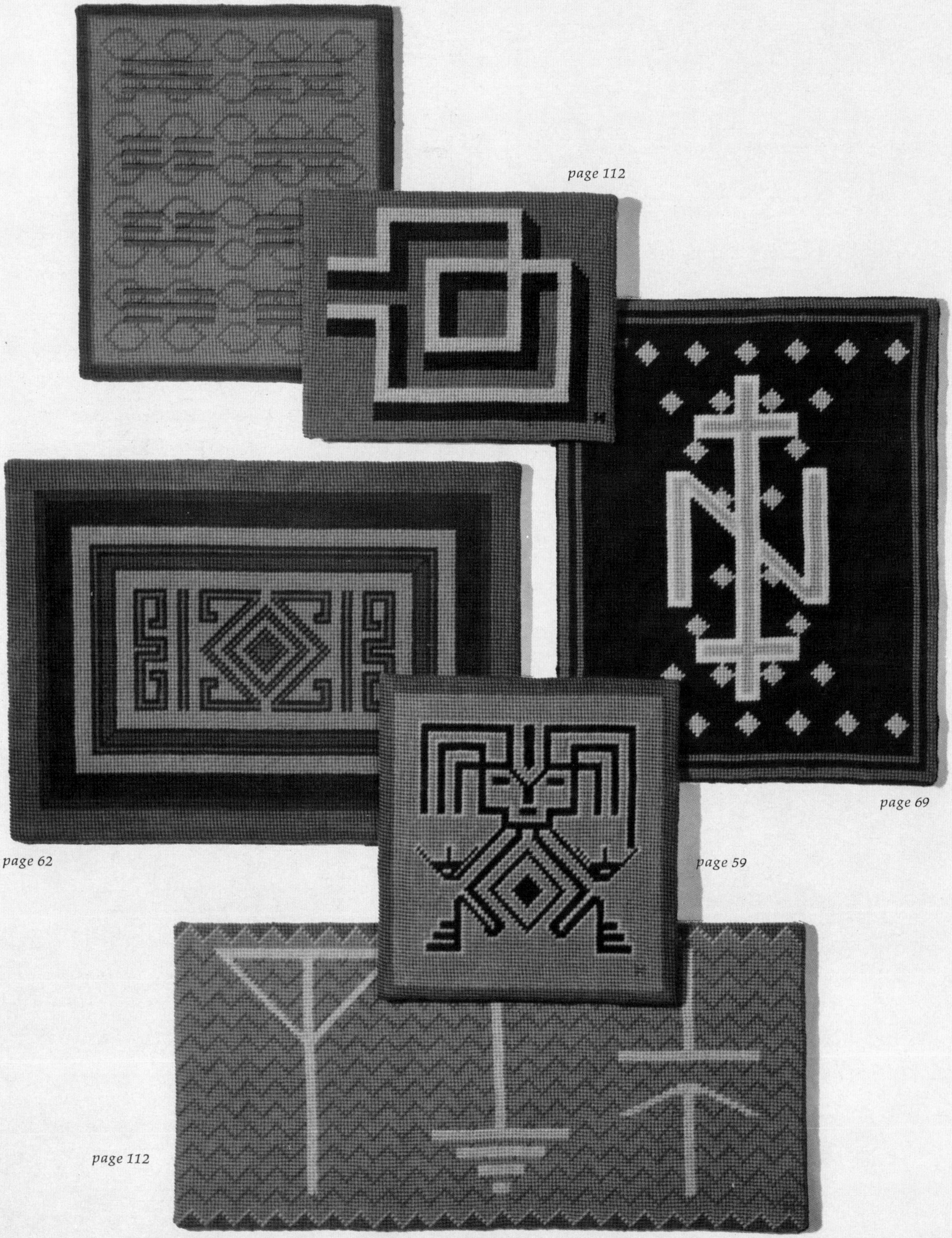

page 26

page 112

page 69

page 62

page 59

page 112

page 77

page 98

page 76

page 61

page 93

page 33

page 52

page 67

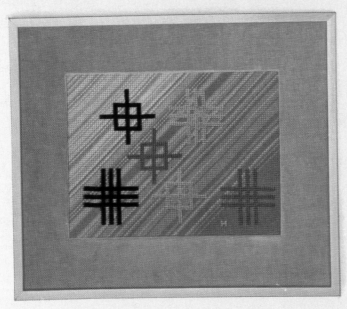

page 104

page 101

One of the most interesting aspects of needlepoint is its wide appeal to both men and women. While few men will boast of sewing a fine seam, there are an increasing number today who are designing and executing beautiful needlepoint. By the way, where and when did the absurd concept of "arts and crafts appropriate to the sexes" start?

It is primarily with men in mind that I have seached for bolder designs and new challenges to the imagination. Floral patterns and whimsical subjects in the manner of the nineteenth century have had their delightful day, I believe, and the time has come to explore ancient and modern sources for material.

The needlepoint canvas itself demands geometric shapes if worked in the early primitive stitch called gros point. My quest for art forms to translate onto canvas in this stitch has led me inevitably to the signs, symbols, and marks of man that have been and continue to be the footnotes of history. The visual forms that man has devised to delineate himself, his thoughts, experiences, and environment can all be translated in dramatic simplicity onto the needlepoint canvas.

We live in an incredibly inventive era, and the creative urge has grown, with more men and women discovering the deep satisfaction of doing their own thing. Those who hesitated to create because of frozen standards of acceptability now seek the high adventure of self-expression. Needlepoint, long restricted to commercial stamped designs offering only the monotonous, mechanical filling-in of empty spaces with predetermined colors, now emerges as one of the most varied and exciting means of that self-expression.

The translation of other art forms into needlepoint takes courage, deliberation, and patience. Indeed, it means severing ties with all that has been secure and predictable in executing someone else's design. But the challenge is wonderful, although at first problems and frustrations seem overwhelming and disappointments may occur far more frequently than success. At this crucial point go into gear—experiment and experiment again until you find the way to express your inner concept. Your patience will carry you beyond discouragement, and suddenly you will find that eye and hand respond to your imagination and their continuity of purpose produces—as if by miracle—a work of your own creation.

For more timid souls the illustrations in this book will provide patterns.

Count the stitches in the photographs and work as you would from graph charts. There are color suggestions with each design, but why not devise your own palette?

I refer to many of these designs as "translations" from other art forms. They are free translations, often taken from small line drawings or black-and-white photographs. Unless the symbolism calls for specific colors, I have chosen my own.

Just as one must think in a foreign language to speak it well, one should think in terms of needlepoint. You will be surprised at how many familiar objects lend themselves to gros point composition and how many landscapes are translatable into the medium. You will search through books and magazines for appropriate ideas, as I have done, and you will enjoy every moment of the treasure hunt.

Going further afield for needlepoint subjects, I have illustrated myths and legends, trying to interpret the style of gesture, the costumes and color palette appropriate to the period of the story. This is a fascinating venture, for some subjects lend themselves to a mosaic technique, others to a stained-glass technique, and still others to the techniques of wood carving, stonework, porcelain, enamel, or weaving.

At the end of this book you will find my own list of sources for the various categories of symbols and motifs shown, but the choice of subjects for needlepoint should be guided by personal interests, and I urge you to set out on your own. To open the door, here are a few subjects that have always intrigued me and that you might explore in needlepoint:

Delft china: Lovely scenes to be translated onto canvas in shades of blue, white, or off-white.

Iron scrollwork: If the scale is large enough, the flowing lines of much of the beautiful New Orleans ironwork can be translated into needlepoint in shades of dark brown and black.

Pennsylvania Dutch motifs: Do not overlook the handsome plate designs, which can be translated into needlepoint in brilliant colors.

Blueprints: Executed in white on blue, these fascinating architectural plans make very ornamental needlepoint pictures and personalized gifts.

Brass rubbings: There is a vogue for brass rubbings today, and they can be worked very effectively on canvas. The attenuated figures and simple devices can be worked in black and old gold.

THE CENTRAL MOTIF

The statement of a needlepoint design is a central motif. The chosen central motif may be a single symbol or a group, a full composition or a detail.

Whether the needlepoint is to be used as a cushion, bag, rug, or seat cover or as a purely ornamental element in the room, the scale of the central motif in relation to the canvas must first be determined to give it visual weight, and then it should be worked in a dominant color or colors. If you wish to throw the central motif into dramatic relief (see pages 33, 49), work the shadow into the background. This may be done by using one color for shadow or gradations of the same color.

BACKGROUNDS AND BORDERS

The last section of designs in this book presents several patterns that can be used in repeats for backgrounds, or if used in a single line, for borders.

These repeated patterns can also be used for scatter rugs when worked in heavy carpet wool on large-mesh canvas.

After the central motif is executed start the background pattern at the center top of the motif (see pages 114–121).

The scale of background and border patterns must be governed by the scale of the central motif, adding to the visual comment without interrupting the basic statement of the composition. Backgrounds and borders may either carry one imaginatively beyond the limits of the canvas (as in the marbleized effect on pages 106, 117), or deliberately confine and intensify the central motif, accenting its importance (pages 47, 108, 109).

When choosing background colors, bear in mind that a simple palette allows for a certain amount of intricacy without creating distraction or loss of purpose. Shades of a single color are very effective, and their use too often overlooked in contemporary design.

EXECUTING DESIGNS

Over six hundred pieces of my work have been executed in the continental stitch, gros point, on #10 penelope canvas. The limitations of this stitch are obvious in handling symmetrical forms, circles, or flowing lines, and in the diminishing perspective of landscape. However, the larger the scale of the composition, the easier to create the illusion of symmetry or curve. And here again the use of shadow will help you (see pages 47, 89, 92). While I have tried more flowing and subtle stitches, I have found far greater satisfaction in translating or devising designs in gros point because of the uniquely primitive effect it produces.

For your first creative effort take such geometric patterns as appear on pages 98 and 99. Become used to the unchanging slant of stich before attempting curving lines. When you find a particularly appealing subject concentrate on its dominant linear features, even though you lose depth of detail. Work the key lines and capture the essence of the design, and with practice the intricacies will no longer worry you. Be patient with yourself as well as with the medium.

When choosing wools, remember that wool in the hank may be deceptively vivid and vibrant, but when worked in juxtaposition with other colors, it may fade into insignificance. As I have learned this lesson through a number of unsuccessful experiments, I suggest that all colors chosen for your composition be worked on a corner of the canvas in consecutive four-stitch squares. This will eliminate unpleasant surprises and unexpected effects, and will keep a balance of tonality.

On the next two pages are photographs of Rudolph Koch's woodcuts from his exciting work *The Book of Signs*. Next to the photographs are pictures of my translations of these signs into needlepoint. The Koch woodcuts in the book are about an inch square. I combined the Day and Night signs and enlarged them into four-inch squares. The upper sign of Day is executed in two shades of yellow, and the lower square of Night in black. The background is worked in shades of gray-blue. Koch's symbol of Winter (somewhat resembling a Japanese torii) is worked in dark brown, with white snowflakes against a background of three shades of gray in a cloud pattern. It is enlarged approximately seven times.

Work, really work on your creative designs, and you will find pleasure commensurate with your efforts. Good luck and happy hours attend your experiments, adventures, and attainments!

DAY AND NIGHT—Woodcuts from *The Book of Signs*, by Rudolph Koch.

Day and Night, Light and Darkness, Openness and Concealment.

DAY AND NIGHT—Hammond needlepoint. The top square, Day, is executed in pale yellow, and the lower square, Night, in black, against a background of four shades of gray-blue in conventionalized cloud pattern.

Actual size: 8½″ x 8⅛″

WINTER—Woodcut from *The Book of Signs*, by Rudolph Koch.

Winter

The symbolism of these signs is not difficult to grasp, illustrating, as they do, the waving and waning of life and, in the case of Winter, protection in a house from cold and snow.

WINTER—Hammond needlepoint, executed in black-brown and four shades of gray.
Actual size: 9″ x 8⅝″

Part Two

THE DESIGNS

Chinese Symbols

According to some authorities the great Chinese sage Confucius (551–479 B.C.) arranged the *I Ching* and wrote its appendices. The sixty-four hexagrams of this book of divination were supposedly developed by the mythological Emperor Fu Hsi from his eight trigrams symbolizing natural phenomena. On the basis of Confucius' having interpreted the hexagrams and written the commentaries, *I Ching* is considered the most important of the Confucian Five Classics.

Because Eastern philosophies are becoming increasingly familiar to the Western world, it seems appropriate to include some of the trigrams and hexagrams with the other Chinese symbols in this section of the book.

The hexagrams may be executed in groups or as single motifs, and the brilliant colors of the Chinese palette—lacquer red, peacock blue, a lighter tone of peacock blue, and mustard yellow, the most familiar of these—can be used. Obviously these symbols are not appropriate for chair seats or cushions, but should be worked as wall hangings or framed pictures.

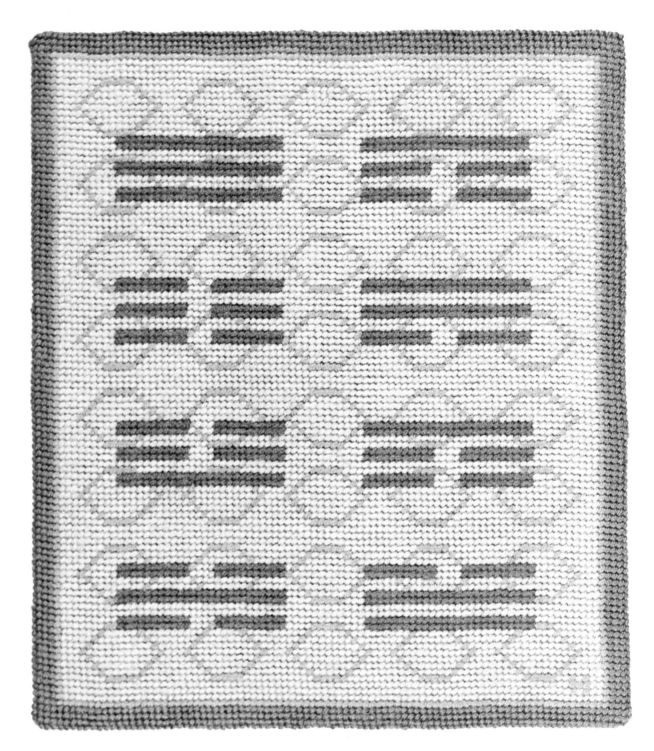

THE EIGHT TRIGRAMS OF FU HSI

Left column, from top: Heaven, Earth, Thunder, Water
Right column, from top: Mountain, Wind, Fire, Marshes

The trigrams are worked in bright red against a background and border of two shades of bright blue.

Actual size: 9¼ " x 10½ "

FOUR TRIGRAMS OF FU HSI AND LANDSCAPE

Because these trigrams represent natural phenomena, I designed my own interpretations of the landscape and superimposed on it the four trigrams that depict, diagonally, Heaven, Mountain, Earth (which is nearly invisible in this photograph, just to the right of the tree trunk), and Water. The trigrams did not have a philosophical significance until they were expanded into the sixty-four hexagrams of the *I Ching* accompanied by the ten *wing*, or appendices, of Confucius.

The trigrams are worked in vermilion against a landscape background of browns and beige.

Actual size: 12¾″ x 11⅝″

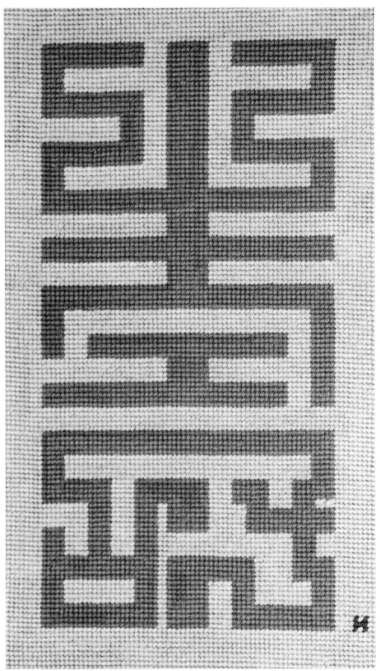

HEXAGRAMS OF THE "I CHING"

Left column, from the top: Khien—Originating; Khwan—Correct; K'an—Sincere; Li—Light.
Right column, from the top: Pi—Concord; Hsiao Khu—Taming Force: Lu—Deliberate Action; T'ai—Peace.

The symbols are worked in white against a background of deep red.

Actual size: 3¾" x 6¼"

THE "SHOU" SYMBOL OF LONGEVITY

One of the many variations of the *shou,* worked in medium red against a medium yellow background.

Actual size: 8¼" x 14½"

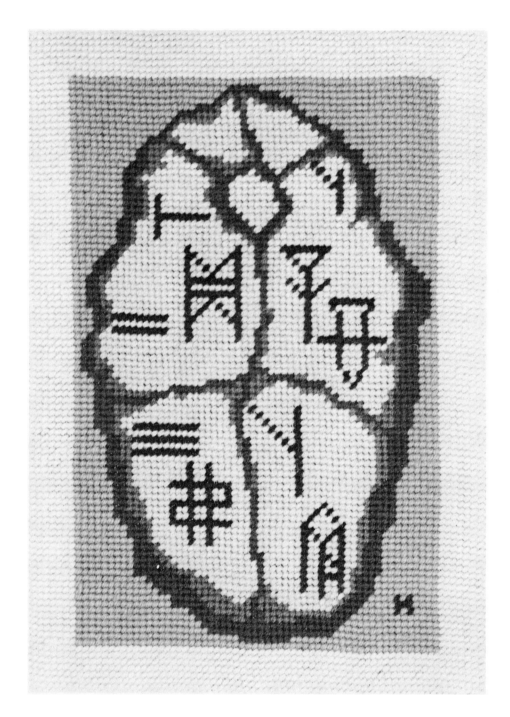

CHINESE ORACLE BONE

Many such oracle bones, dating from the Shan or Yin dynasty (1766–1122 B.C.), have been found in Honan province. They were inscribed with symbols from the Chinese Bronze Civilization and placed on a fire, and omens were read from the resulting pattern of cracks.

The motif is worked in three shades of brown and beige against a background of Chinese blue, and the border is of medium yellow.

Actual size: 7½" x 10¾"

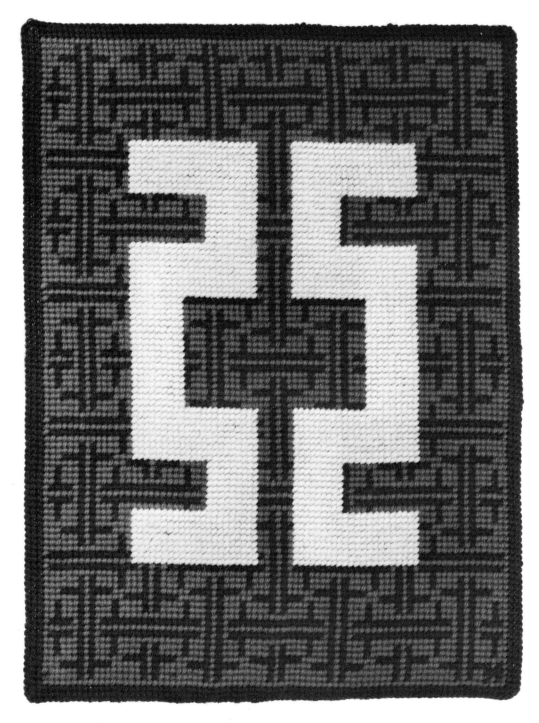

SYMBOL OF DISTINCTION

An element of a Chinese imperial robe of the Kuang Hsu period (1875–1908), taken from a photograph in *Robes of the Forbidden City*, by Alan Priest, Curator Emeritus of Far Eastern Art at the Metropolitan Museum of Art.

The symbol is worked in light gold against a Chinese textile background of the same period executed in two shades of red.

Actual size: 8⅝″ x 11½″

Tibetan Symbols

Today this country lives in the courageous hearts of its exiled people, in the minds of students of Eastern philosophies, and in the imagination of anyone who has seen photographs of Lhasa and its once beautiful monasteries and mountain fastnesses.

THE TIBETAN SHOU SYMBOL OF LONGEVITY

The central motif is worked in bright yellow against a background of two shades of bright blue. As I prefer the restricted palette, the shading behind the central motif is the same blue as the border.

Actual size: 9½" x 11¼"

"PALBU," THE TIBETAN SYMBOL OF THE EIGHTH BUDDHIST SYMBOL

In Tibet the eighth Buddhist symbol is known as the "Endless Knot" symbolizing love and devotion.

The interlaced squares are deep red bordered in gold, the shadows and border are of medium bright blue, and the background is of light bright blue.

Actual size: 12" x 9⅝"

COLORS OF THE FOUR CORNERS OF THE WORLD

According to Faber Birren's *Color Psychology and Color Therapy*, the Tibetan directional colors are: north—yellow; south—blue; east—white and west—red. The Tibetans conceived the world as a high mountain called *sumur*, pyramidal in shape but without a pointed apex.

Actual size: 10¾" x 11"

THE WORD "TIBET"

The symbols are worked in bright yellow against alternate striated squares of dark and medium bright blue, and light and pale bright blue.

Actual size: 12¼" x 9¼"

Near East Symbols

Naturally these symbols spread across Europe, their forms often slightly altered and their significance changed.

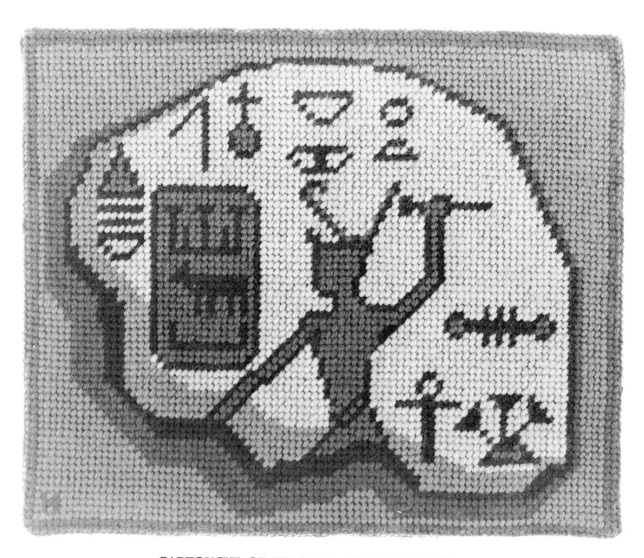

CARTOUCHE OF SHABAKA, KING OF EGYPT

A cartouche is a seal and this is the seal of Shabaka, King of Egypt (712–700 B.C.), thought to be the "So" mentioned in the Second Book of Kings (xvii.4) as having received ambassadors from Hoshea, King of Israel. He belonged to the XXVth (Ethiopian) dynasty and the capital of his domain was Napata. Here the king is shown wearing the red cap, *teshr*, holding a mace in one hand and reaching with the other for the hair of a prisoner he is about to behead.

The design is outlined in dark brown, shaded in medium brown, and executed in beige against a two-tone bright blue background, with a border of the darker blue.

Actual size: 9½″ x 7½″

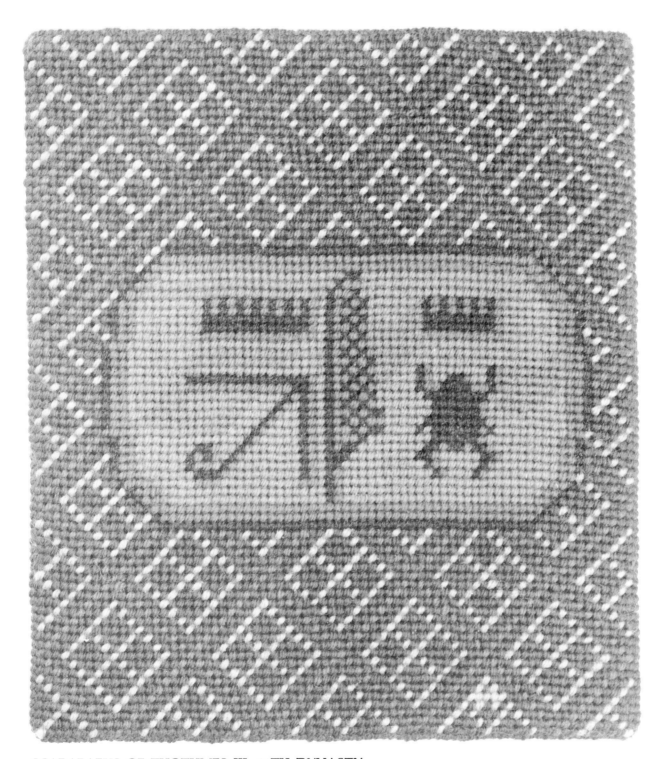

SCARABAEUS OF THOTHMES III, 18TH DYNASTY

This scarabaeus—scrab or seal—belonged to Thothmes III, one of the greatest
Egyptian kings. He was of the 18th dynasty, and ruled jointly with his wife
and half sister, Hatshepsut, from about 1501 to 1481 B.C. He ruled alone from
1481 to 1447 B.C., leading seventeen campaigns into Asia and conquering Meso-
potamia. His architectural legacy is important, for he enlarged the Temple of
Amen at Karnak and restored the temples of Heliopolis, Memphis, and Abydos,
among others.

The figures are worked in dark brown on henna, and the background is of
quartered lozenges worked in three shades of moss green.

Actual size: 7½″ x 8½″

FRAGMENT OF A CASTLE BY A RIVER AT KOUYUNJIK

This is the title of a black-and-white drawing that I found in the book *Discoveries Among the Ruins of Nineveh and Babylon*, by Austen Layard. The book is an account of the findings of the second expedition made by the trustees of the British Museum. As a free translation into needlepoint, the patterns to the left of the ornamented door represent trees, the fish emphasize the river.

The design is outlined in dark brown and worked in beige, against a background of medium gray-green.

Actual size: 9⅛″ x 8¼″

OPPOSITE:

THE NAME OF THE ASSYRIAN SUN GOD, SHAMASH

From the cuneiform king's tablets, discovered at Nimrud.

The design is worked in dark brown against a bright yellow background, with corners and borders of medium henna.

Actual size: 12½″ x 5½″

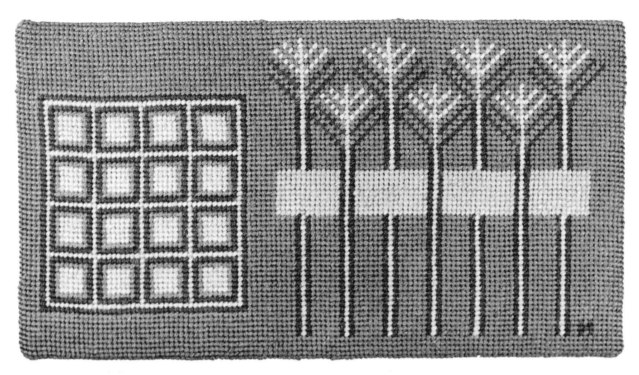

PRIMITIVE GARDEN OF THE DEAD, EGYPT, 18TH DYNASTY c. 1580 B.C.

The squares represent a vegetable garden, and the band crossing the seven sycamore trees represents a water tank.

The squares are outlined in dark brown and worked in two shades of gold. The symbol for the water tank is worked in henna, and the sycamores are light gold, outlined in dark brown. The background is medium blue.

Actual size: 13″ x 7″

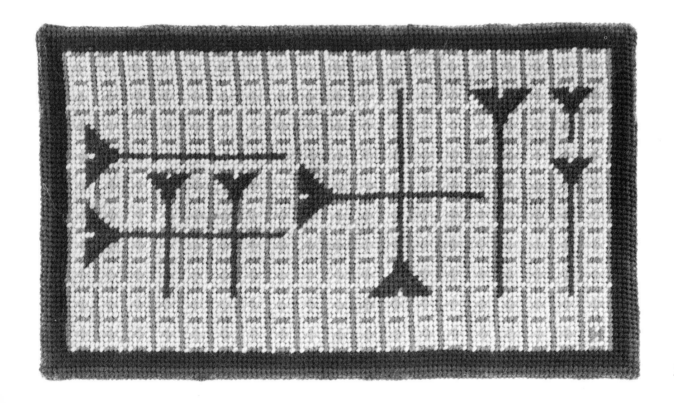

THE NAME "NINEVEH" IN CUNEIFORM

The city was mentioned in the Old Testament and may have been in existence in the 18th Egyptian dynasty.

The symbols are worked in dark gold against a diapered background of three lighter shades of gold. The inner border is royal purple and the outer border dark gold.

Actual size: 12¼″ x 7″

Hebrew Symbols

The strong and striking symbols of the Jewish people, so rich in feeling and meaning, are perhaps the most exciting and challenging to work in needlepoint.

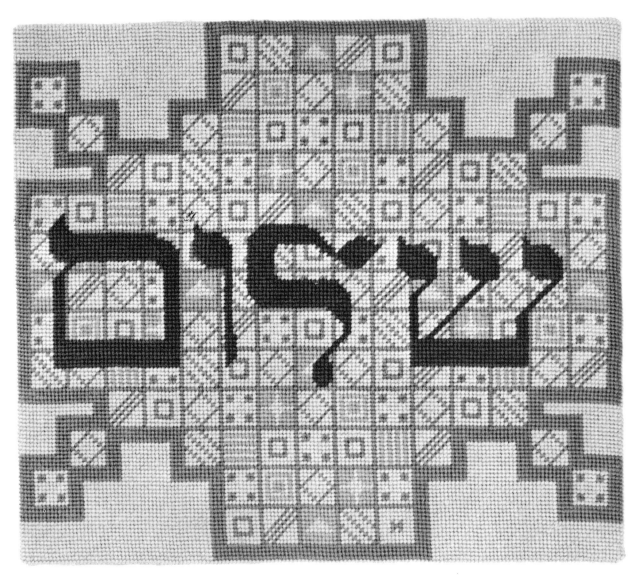

"SHALOM"

Forms of the word "shalom" appear in all the Semitic languages, in Hebrew stemming from *shalem*, which means "complete." Originally a question—*Shalom l'cha?* or *Shalom aleicha* ("Are you all right?" or "How are you?")—it is a universal greeting that communicates good will and has many connotations: peace, quiet, tranquility, safety, welfare, health, contentment, good condition, success, comfort, greetings.

The "shalom" is worked in bright blue, the background in shades of beige.

Actual size: 15⅞″ x 13⅜″

THE THREE CROWNS

The crown is a symbol that figures prominently in both Jewish and Christian religions; here are the three crowns from the Old Testament.

Each crown is bright gold, worked on a background of purple hues.

Actual size: 4½″ x 5⅞″

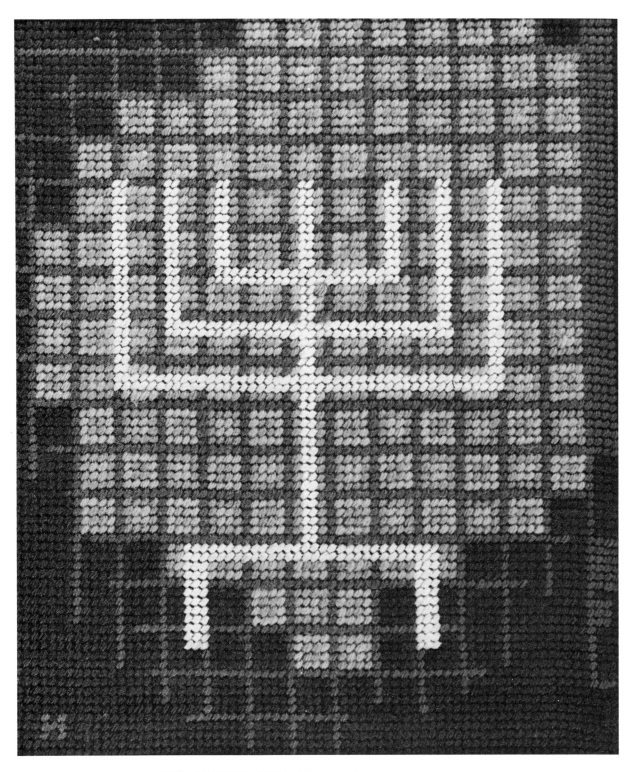

THE SEVEN-BRANCHED MENORAH

In the Bible (Exodus 25.31–40) God directed Moses to make a seven-branched menorah in the desert. The word "menorah" has as its root "noor," meaning "light" or "fire." The menorah has been interpreted as the Sacred Tree, or Tree of Life, on which lights hung. As it manifests God's mercy and forgiveness, the menorah concentrates all Jewish hopes.

The menorah is worked in gold on a checked background of two shades of blue.

Actual size: 7¼" x 8⅞"

THE SEVEN-BRANCHED MENORAH

Another version of the Menorah, worked in gold against a purple background.

Actual size: 12¼″ x 12¼″

"BE STRONG OF GOOD COURAGE"

The Hebrew letters are worked in bright blue against a background of three shades of old gold.

Actual size: 18½″ x 5½″

"TRUE LIFE"

The Hebrew letters are worked in medium blue against a three-toned gold background.

Actual size: 12¾″ x 11½″

Christian Symbols

Over three hundred books have been written about the cross, but its origins are still a matter of conjecture. Its existence, four thousand years before the birth of Christ, is recorded, and in various forms it has been found in all ancient cultures and on all continents.

In his book *Designs and Devices*, Clarence P. Hornung suggests dividing the study of this symbol into three historical periods: the first from 4000 B.C. to the Christian era; the second from the early Christian era to A.D. 900; and the third encompassing the Middle Ages and the Crusades, during which periods many of the variants of the cross were developed.

THE ICTHUS, MONOGRAM OF JESUS CHRIST

The symbols are worked in four shades of gray-green.

Actual size: 9¾" x 13⅝"

CHRISMON, MONOGRAM OF JESUS CHRIST

The central motif is worked in two shades of gold, and the background and frames in five shades of blue.

Actual size: 9½″ x 10⅛″

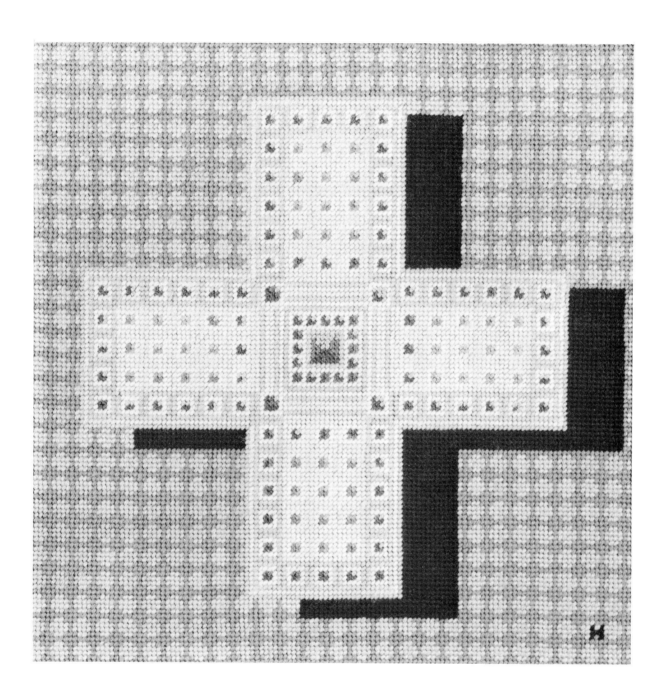

THE GREEK CROSS, OR CROSS IMMISSA QUADRATE

The cross is worked in three shades of old gold and is studded with gems in three shades of bright red and three shades of green, with the background diapered in light green against medium green. The shadow is dark green.

Actual size: 13¾″ x 13¾″

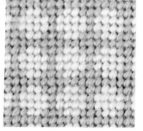

CROSSES OF SAINTS

Left: St. Sylvester; St. Julian.
Center: St. Patrick; St. George; St. Anthony.
Right: St. Peter; St. Ethelred.

The shields and crosses are worked in two shades of old gold and the background is checked in two shades of olive green. The dark shadows are worked in dark olive green, and the border shadows in medium olive green.

Actual size: 9¾″ x 14″

THE PAPAL CROSS

The cross is worked in two shades of gold against a mauve background with deeper mauve shadow. Gold corners are studded with turquoise matrix.

Actual size: 7½″ x 10″

THE LOTHARINGIAN CROSS

The ancient cross of Lorraine

Worked in medium brown and beige, the cross is outlined in dark brown. The background is executed in three shades of red.

Actual size: 7½″ x 7⅜″

53

American Indian Symbols

Among many early civilizations the symbols are predominantly of magic, destruction, doom, and death. It is therefore a joy to work some of the symbols of the Navajo Indians, which seem to reflect a spiritual peace and the clear skies that arched their world.

FOUR NAVAJO SYMBOLS

From the top: Sky Band—Leading to Happiness; Distant Mountains; Big Mountain—Abundance; Fence—Guard of Good Luck.

Colors: Sky Band; deep henna; Distant Mountains, dark green; Big Mountain, medium green; Fence, dark brown; the sky, bright blue; the earth background in lower half of the picture, faded ocher.

Actual size: 9⅝″ x 11⅞″

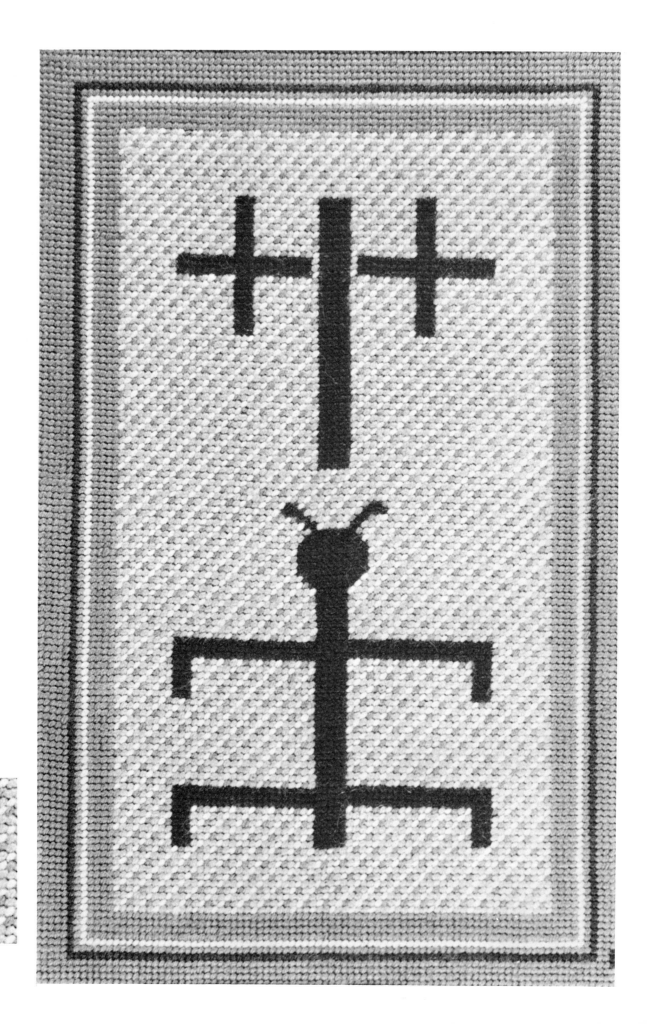

SEVEN NAVAJO SYMBOLS

Swastika—Good Luck; Tepee—Temporary Home; Cactus—Desert; Morning Star—Guidance; Running Water—Constant Life; Arrow—Protection; Fence—Guard of Good Luck.

Colors: Tepee: off-white and black; Fence: blue, in two shades; double Morning Star: medium yellow; Running Water: medium blue; Arrow: dark brown; Cactus: two shades of bright green; Swastika: dark brown; worked against a background of deep sand-color.

Actual size: 13¾″ x 11⅝″

OPPOSITE:

THE DRAGON FLY

The two central designs are tribal representations of the dragonfly, thought to be a supernatural being warning men of danger. At top, the symbol of the Dakota tribe; at bottom, that of the Moki Indians. Both tribes are from Arizona.

Both motifs are worked in dark brown against a background of diagonal lines in three shades of bright green, and bordered in three shades of the same green.

Actual size: 9⅜″ x 14⅞″

Mexican Flat
and Cylindrical Stamps

Baked-clay stamps, flat or cylindrical, were used decoratively to incise pottery or to imprint cloth, paper, or skins. They have been found in the ancient cultures of the Mediterranean region as well as in the western hemisphere. Following are some of the bold stamp designs from ancient Mexico.

A CYLINDRICAL STAMP

Conventionalized human figure, from Guerrero

The central motif is worked in dark brown bordered with medium gold, against a background of gray-green. The design is bordered with a darker shade of gray-green.

Actual size: 8⅝″ x 9″

A MEXICAN BIRD

The central motif is outlined in dark brown, the eye worked in bright red, and the wings and body in two shades of bright blue. The background is unevenly striped in two shades of yellow-green.

Actual size: 9″ x 10½″

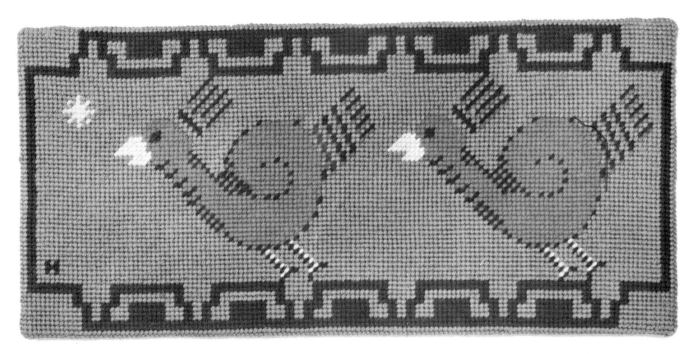

TWO BIRDS

The birds are outlined in dark red and worked in bright red, with medium yellow beaks and legs. The background is bright green, and the border is a Mexican pattern worked in dark green with a dark red rectangular center.

Actual size: 14¾″ x 6⅝″

SECTION OF A RITUAL STAFF

The central motif is outlined in dark brown and worked in bright blue against a symmetrical striping of dark yellow and medium yellow.

Actual size: 9⅜″ x 11″

GEOMETRIC DESIGN

The center of the central motif is olive green, and all the central motif is worked in bright henna, outlined in dark brown. The background is bright blue. The borders are medium henna, olive green, dark henna, dark olive green, and medium olive green.

Actual size: 15″ x 10⅝″

MEXICAN CYLINDRICAL STAMP DESIGN

The design is worked in alternate patterns of bright red and dark red with dark brown horizontal bars edged in dark yellow. The background is of bright yellow.

Actual size: 12⅜″ x 9¾″

African Symbols

The simple beauty of African art forms has long fascinated me, and it was inevitable that I should try to translate into needlepoint the inch-high metal birds of my modest collection of Ashanti gold weights, the small brass weights used to measure out the gold dust and nuggets on which the Ashanti economy was based. I worked them against backgrounds or with borders of African designs, and I did not try to render the small figures in the round, but attempted rather to preserve their bold statement.

You may wish to turn to Margaret Webster Plass's book *African Miniatures, Goldweights of the Ashanti* (New York: Praeger Publishers, 1967) for further inspirations.

64

ASHANTI GOLD WEIGHT

The bird is worked in shades of gold against an African geometric background
of four shades of olive green.

Actual size: 11″ x 14½″

OPPOSITE:

ASHANTI GOLD WEIGHT

The bird is worked in shades of gold against a dregs-of-wine red background,
bordered in brown and off-white.

Actual size: 13⅞″ x 11⅞″

Hobo Signs

In Stewart H. Holbrook's *The Story of American Railroads* hoboes and other roamers are thus defined: "A hobo works and wanders, a tramp dreams and wanders, and a bum drinks and wanders."

These three types of migrants took to the rails in the confusion and social dislocation following the Civil War. By the nineties there were some 60,000 riding the rods beneath the railway cars, or the blinds connecting them, in quest of freedom or adventure.

As late as the 1920s one could spot the glow of their campfires in the desolate wastes of the Dakota badlands, in the lonely sweeps of Kansas prairies, or in the opalescent snows of the Sierra passes. Only with the mass production of automobiles and the increased volume of air traffic did the classical fraternity of hoboes forsake the rails.

They have left us not only a legacy of songs and ballads but a pictographic language. These signs, scrawled on fences, sidewalks, or gateposts, were practical guides to all members of the fraternity, depicting homes of affluence and sources of handouts or patrolled and guarded areas of danger.

Unfortunately only a few of these signs have survived, but their place in the vast field of communications cannot be overlooked in the history of our nineteenth-century frontiers.

HOBO SIGNS

Upper left: Wealth; *Upper right:* Afraid; *Center:* Guarded House; *Lower left:* Danger; *Lower right:* Jail.

The signs are worked in black against a background of four shades of gray-green. It would also be appropriate to work them in off-white against a ground of grays.

Actual size: 9¼″ x 7½″

Stonemasons' Marks

In A.D. 1268 Étienne Boileau, who was appointed by Louis IX of France to reform the government of the city of Paris, drew up the "*Livres des Métiers*," in which reference was made to the masons' guilds. Out of three hundred mentioned, sixty-two asserted freedom. George Gordon Coulton, the English historian, believes that "freemason" meant "worker in freestone." According to early building accounts, freemasons were a separate body from the rough-masons or hand-hewers.

Freemasons were building craftsmen, and they often worked in large numbers, traveling from job to job without fixed headquarters. When they worked on church structures they were often housed in adjacent monasteries, but when they were employed on temporal buildings they had to live within the community according to a strict code of self-government.

The first documentary evidence of masons' marks is found in the Torgau Articles of 1530. The mark of a stonemason was conferred on him on the termination of his apprenticeship as journeyman. It was granted by the master of his masonic lodge, and was derived from the mother figure of that particular lodge. When a stonemason became a master of his vocation he was allowed to enclose his mark within a shield.

Originally masonic lodges were controlled by the Church, and even when they gained dominion over their own societies they stressed the importance of Christian principles and ethics. Ill conduct deprived a mason of his mark and membership in his lodge.

It was not until A.D. 1717 that the institution of Grand Lodge evolved, and Freemasonry became a national institution, losing its ancient and close connection with operative masonry.

STONEMASON'S MARK FROM A GOTHIC EDIFICE

The center motif is worked in two shades of yellow. The dark blue background
diapered in light blue and the border in two shades of blue are my additions.

Actual size: 11″ x 13½″

STONEMASON'S MARK FROM A GOTHIC EDIFICE

The motif is worked in black-brown against a marbleized background of moss greens.

Actual size: 8″ x 7⅝″

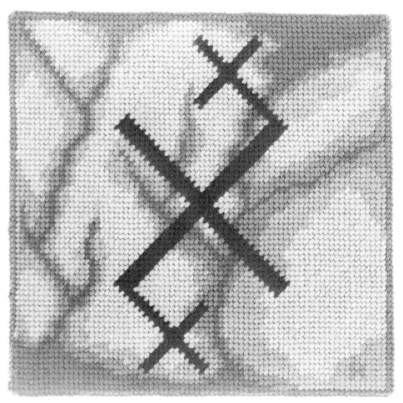

ROMAN STONEMASON'S MARK

The central motifs are worked in dark brown against a green marbleized background.

Actual size: 9″ x 8½″

STONEMASON'S MARK FROM A GOTHIC EDIFICE

The central motif is executed in dark brown against a diapered background
worked in two shades of gray-blue.

Actual size: $7\frac{1}{8}$″ x $8\frac{3}{4}$″

BYZANTINE STONEMASON'S MARK

The stonemason's mark is worked in dark brown on a medium yellow background.

Actual size: 5½″ x 5¼″

STONEMASON'S MARK FROM VINCENNES, FRANCE

The motif is worked in two shades of yellow against a checked background of two shades of plum color.

Actual size: 6″ x 7½″

MASONS' MARKS FROM THE TAJ MAHAL, AGRA, INDIA

The incised symbols and the marbleized background are executed in shades of gray.

Actual size: 12 ⅜″ x 11″

MARK OF JODOCUS TAUCHEN, STONEMASON, SILESIA, 1450

For centuries Silesia was a part of Poland. It belonged to Bohemia in the fourteenth century and to the Holy Roman Empire in 1478, and was seized by Prussia from Austria in 1742.

The design is worked in dark brown, with a marbleized background of four shades of gray.

Actual size: 10¾″ x 11¾″

House Marks
and Holding Marks

The earliest form of house mark was notched in straight lines, the curved and ornate designs being of a much later date. This fact is also applicable to holding marks, which were used on movable properties. According to Rudolph Koch (*The Book of Signs*), these were snipped into the ears of domestic animals, clipped out of the coats of horses, painted on sheep, and cut into the upper bills of swans. They were proof of ownership in litigations, and as technologies developed, their use spread.

HOUSE MARK

The family symbol of the cross is here shown with four modifications of four sons of the family.

The crosses are worked in bright yellow and the modifications in a darker yellow. The background of squares is worked in three shades of henna.

Actual size: 10¼″ x 11⅛″

HOUSE MARK

Top: Symbol of the House
Bottom: Windmill, Key, Chevron.

According to Rudolph Koch, house marks were at first the individual signs of peasant proprietors, and designated their holdings. Later they became personal symbols, which eventually developed into trademarks. In some heraldic manuals the chevron represents the roof of a house, which it certainly suggests visually.

The four separate house marks are worked in dark brown against a checked background of three shades of henna.

Actual size: 11⅞″ x 9″

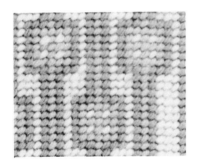

HOLDING MARK OF PETER VISCHER, 1455–1529, GERMAN BELL FOUNDER

It should be noted that holding marks, trademarks, and merchants' marks frequently used the sign of Hermes (which resembles our Arabic number "4"), straight, reversed or inverted, for approximately a century and a half.

The central motif is worked in dark brown against a pattern of three shades of yellow.

Actual size: 12″ x 10¾″

Commerce

MERCHANTS' MARKS,
OCCUPATIONAL MARKS, AND COUNTER MARKS

Little is known of most of the merchants who devised their marks. But let us think of the adventures, the heartbreaks, the successes summarized in these emblems. Let us think of the artisans and merchants working long hours in their little shops opening on narrow, rat-infested alleyways. Let us remember the courageous souls who traveled the stormy trade routes of the Baltic and the Mediterranean, and who ventured across the ominous expanses of the Atlantic and Pacific oceans.

Probably one of the important advances of our century is our realization that we have "neighbors" distant in time and space. Neighbors who lived, who worked and died, even as we. Neighbors with different customs but the same problems of mortality. If you think of the merchants of long ago, you will have pleasure and excitement in translating their symbols into needlepoint.

The marks of long-dead merchants can be seen in the commemorative carvings of English country churches. An amazing number incorporate the sign of Hermes, which resembles our Arabic number "4." Those delineated on shields might be master merchants, as in the stonemasons' marks.

The counter marks denote the quality of goods in a symbolism probably not understood by the customer, but familiar to the trade.

In substance, the development of these marks shows how little the necessities of man have changed throughout the centuries. Some of these are symbolic and some pictographic, but to date scholars have not agreed upon their chronological precedence. In all I find the beauty of simplicity.

MARK OF HANS SACHS, GERMAN SHOEMAKER AND MEISTERSINGER AND POET (A.D. 1494–1576)

The emblem is worked in dark brown against a geometric background executed in three shades of bright blue. The central motif is so strong that the ornate background did not interrupt the statement.

Actual size: 8¼″ x 12⅞″

14TH CENTURY MERCHANT'S MARK

The central motif is worked in bright yellow, and the wave patterns in two shades of gray-blue, against a light gray-blue background.

Actual size 11⅞″ x 13¼″

ESSEX MERCHANT'S MARK

Mark of John Beriffe, who died in A.D. 1536 and was commemorated in Brightlinsea Church, Essex, England.

The motif is worked in light gray, the shield in medium gray, and the motif's shadow in darker gray. The background is of stripes of contrasting grays, with the shadow of the shield executed in black.

Actual size: 9½″ x 11⅝″

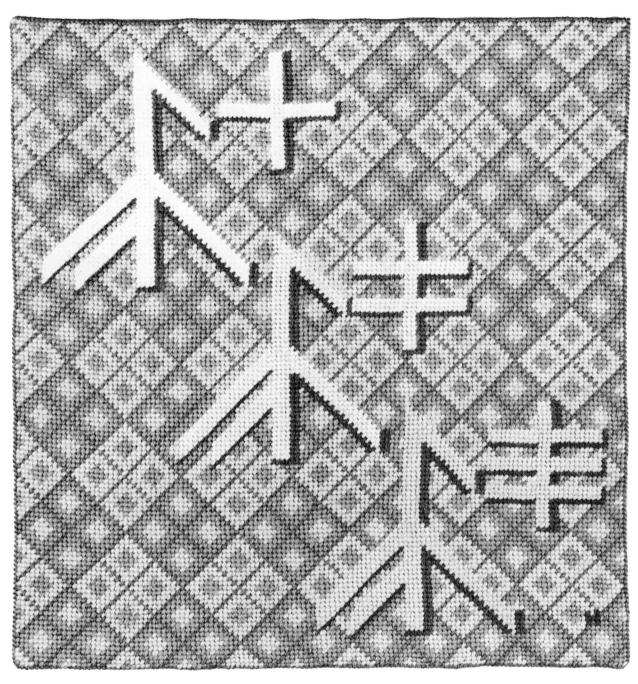

COUNTER MARKS

In medieval times such marks were used to grade marketable goods. The left symbol is the owner's trademark; the crosses denote first, second, and third grades. The secret codes of merchandising still exist.

The top symbol and cross are worked in light yellow, the middle symbol and cross in medium yellow, and the third symbol and cross in dark yellow. The background is diapered in three shades of blue-green.

Actual size: 13⅛″ x 13½″

OCCUPATIONAL MARKS

Left to right: Merchant, Mercer, Grocer, Brewer.

The marks are worked in dark brown against a subtle lozenge pattern outlined in light blue; background of medium blue and shadows of dark blue.

Actual size: 11⅞″ x 12″

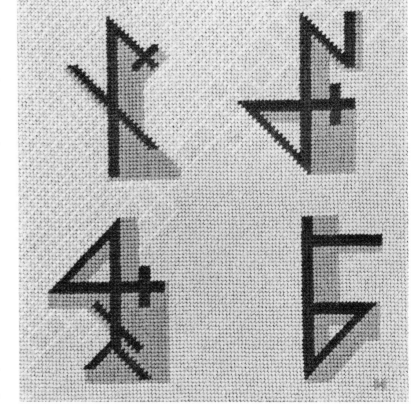

BELOW:

14TH CENTURY MERCHANT'S MARK

The central motif is worked in bright yellow against a background of three shades of gray-blue.

Actual size: 14⅝″ x 12⅛″

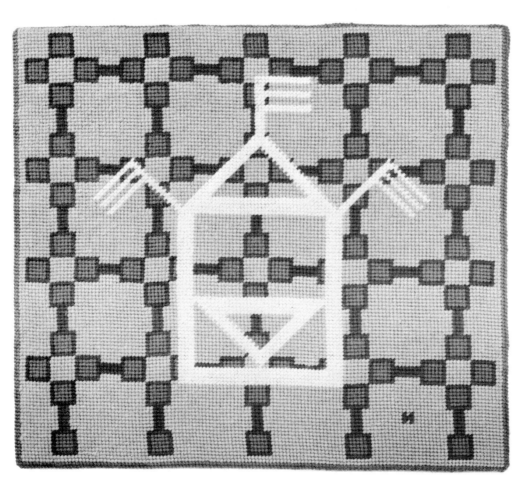

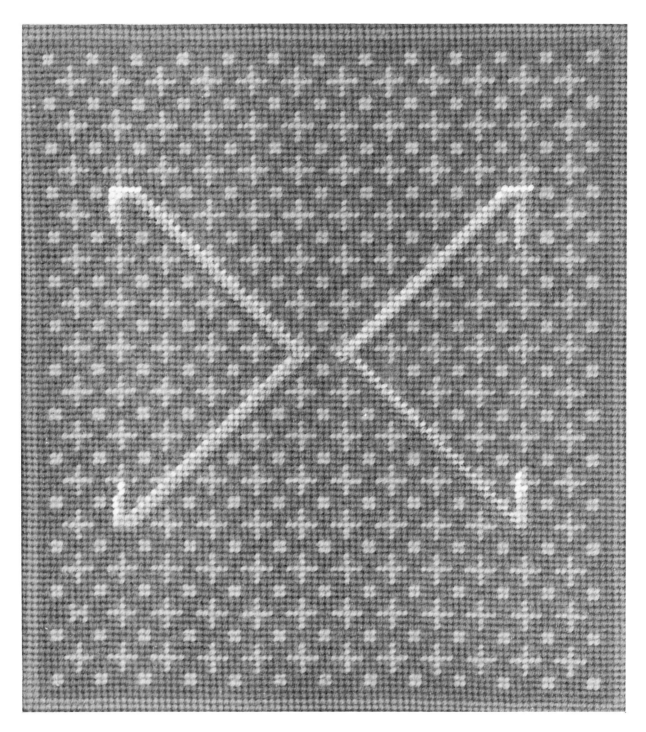

CLOTHWORKER'S MARK

These tenterhooks (sharp, hooked nails used in stretching cloth on the tenter) were part of the grave slab of Richard Davy, who died in A.D. 1514 and is buried in the church in Nayland, England.

The motifs are worked in shades of gray against a red diapered background.

Actual size: 10″ x 11⅛″

16TH CENTURY MERCHANT'S MARK

The central motif is worked in henna against a square-and-line pattern in olive greens.

Actual size: 8⅝″ x 13¼″

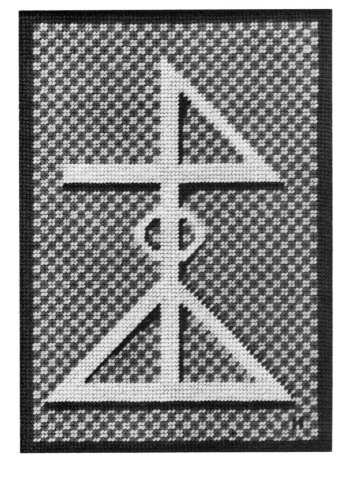

SUFFOLK MERCHANT'S MARK

Commemorative carved mark of Thomas Walle, who lived in A.D. 1520, discovered on the battlements of Walle Chapel, Grundisburgh Church, Suffolk, England.

The motif is executed in medium yellow, with a diapered background of light and medium brown, the shadows and border being of dark brown.

Actual size: 8⅝″ x 12″

Heraldic Beasts

The longer I have studied heraldry, the greater my conviction that it is the basic shorthand of history. An escutcheon and its bearings can be read as clearly as the printed words on a page; its significance cannot be as easily confused as the written word in translation.

So for those who care to wander through the picturesque corridors of England's past, I recommend execution of heraldic beasts in needlepoint.

THE LEOPARD

Part of the armorial bearings of the Worshipful Company of Goldsmiths.

The motif is outlined in dark brown and worked in gold against a red diapered background.

Actual size: 9⅝" x 9⅝"

THE OWL

This is part of the crest of the Worshipful Company of Solicitors, which was constituted on the pattern of an ancient guild, and which received a grant of livery from the Court of Aldermen in May 1944.

The bird is worked in soft gray and brown against a background of gold and bright red.

Actual size: 9" x 9½"

THE LIZARD

This is the crest of the Worshipful Company of Ironmongers, who are recorded as an organized body in A.D. 1300. The lizards may have represented salamanders, which early naturalists believed able to survive the hottest fire.

The wreath (or platform on which the lizards stand) is blue, red, and silver, and the green lizards are bound by a red chain. The background is light blue.

Actual size:
9¾" x 9½"

Armorers' Marks

Translating armorers' marks into needlepoint does not seem to me as illogical as it might first appear to be. Surely some long-forgotten housewife worked her husband's trademark for the mantelpiece or as a wall hanging for a long-forgotten Christmas of the past.

But usually armorers' marks were found incised on the inner surface of small shoulder shields called ailetes, or on the heel of long, pointed-toed foot guards called *A la Poulaine solerets*, or on the haft of a crossbow known as an arbalest. They were also placed on the steel-plated front and back peaks of war saddles, called *arciones*, and on archers' rings, and inside the collared, closed helmets depicted so often in heraldic crests, named armets.

15TH CENTURY AUSTRIAN ARMORER'S MARK

The bird is worked in deep yellow against a background diapered in two shades
of green. The shadow is dark green.

Actual size: 11¼" x 10½"

TORTOISE: A MOVABLE BATTERING RAM

Testudine, the tortoise battering ram, offered protection to the men working in it. The design is translated into needlepoint from an illustration in George Cameron Stone's *A Glossary of the Construction, Decoration and Use of Arms and Armor.*

The battering ram is worked in shades of brown, with the tortoise's head in green. The fortification under attack is worked in shades of brown, the lettering in dark brown shaded in medium blue, the sky in three shades of blue cloud-pattern, and the foreground in shades of faded olive green.

Actual size: 12¾″ x 8⅜″

Magic Signs

Are you superstitious? Do you have a "lucky day," a "lucky number," or perhaps a "lucky piece"? Would you rather not "walk under a ladder," or "throw a hat on the bed," or "see the new moon through glass"?

Here are a few of the designs I have found in my search for symbols. The background research is basically encompassed in the "Source Books" section that begins on page 127.

AMULET FROM THE BOOK OF RAZIEL

According to E. A. Wallis Budge, in his book *Amulets and Talismans*, this Hebrew amulet was made to give the wearer success in business, and was written on parchment and worn on the left arm. On it are four permutations of the letters "SLH" which mean "make to prosper," and the name of God, "YH9 = YHWH." The inscriptions on amulets were often written in the Kabbalistic forms of the letters of the Hebrew alphabet.

The amulet is worked in brown shades on a background of two shades of yellow. The border is gray-blue, with light blue stars.

Actual size: 14″ x 8½″

OPPOSITE:

THE UDJATTI AMULET

The Udjatti, or "Two Eyes," dating from the Egyptian dynastic period, was considered a powerful symbol against evil, and not only was used as an amulet but was painted on the prows of ships and on coffins and sarcophagi.

The central motif is outlined in dark brown and worked in three shades of gold. The border is worked in two shades of faded green.

Actual size: 10⅝″ x 6″

THE TWELVE HOUSES OF HEAVEN ACCORDING TO THE MEDIEVAL KABBALISTS

I. House of Life; II. House of Wealth; III. House of Brethren; IV. House of Kinsfolk; V. House of Children; VI. House of Slaves; VII. House of Marriage; VIII. House of Death; IX. House of Charity; X. House of Glory; XI. House of Peace (Happiness); XII. House of Hatred.

The design is executed in two shades of old gold against a deep purple background.

Actual size: 10⅜" x 10"

THE BATRA GIWARGIS AMULET

This Ethiopian amulet depicts King Solomon and his wife, Balkis, Queen of Sheba. The king is seated (left), with a crescent moon above his head, and the queen is standing, masking her mouth in the Oriental fashion with a portion of her outer garment. Above her head is the sun. The amulet is described as "Salomon mesla be'esitu," or "Solomon and his wife."

The central motif is worked in shades of gold, with the king's robe of purple, and the queen's robe of red with a gold and dull green outer garment. The border is dark blue, the inner rectangle medium blue.

Actual size: 13¼″ x 11¼″

94

THE DIVINE GOOSE, OR GREAT CACKLER

This Egyptian amulet of the goose that laid the cosmic egg probably dates from the New Kingdom.

The design is outlined in dark brown and worked in four shades of gold against a faience-blue background.

Actual size: 9½″ x 9⅜″

SAINT GEORGE, THE MARTYR OF LYDDA, SPEARING THE GREAT DRAGON

According to E. A. Wallis Budge, this Syriac amulet was a safeguard against fear and trembling. The power of such amulets was in the varied forms of the name of God and in the ten words of God that produced the universe. In this power the Syriac charms are identical with those of the Hebrews in their Kabbalah, the Egyptian Christians, the Abyssinians, the Samaritans, and the Arabs.

The saint wears a dull red robe, the horse is beige, and the serpent is worked in shades of green. The background and shadows are in shades of blue.

Actual size: 9" x 9⅛"

Astrological Signs

The contemporary astrological signs are handsome and familiar, so I have sought a few less well-known symbols to translate into needlepoint.

THE CHARACTER OF MERCURY

According to Cornelius Heinrich Agrippa, called Agrippa von Nettesheim, German physician, theologian, and student of the occult (A.D. 1485–1535).

The central motif is worked in dark purple and outlined in two shades of old gold. The background is gray-blue, and the border medium gray-blue.

Actual size: 12⅛" x 8¾"

THE CHARACTER OF THE PLANET MARS

According to Cornelius Heinrich Agrippa

The central motif is worked in old gold with a dark red border against a geometric background of two shades of blue.

Actual size: 9½" x 11"

THE CHARACTER OF THE PLANET JUPITER

According to Cornelius Heinrich Agrippa

The two triangles are worked in two shades of old gold against a background of squares in three shades of gray-blue.

Actual size: 9⅝" x 9⅝"

THE CHARACTER OF LUNA (THE MOON)

According to Cornelius Heinrich Agrippa

The central motif is worked in two shades of old gold against a background of dark gray-blue and medium gray-blue.

Actual size: 9½" x 9½"

Ancient Chemical Signs

As Rudolph Koch wrote in *The Book of Signs:* "There are many [of these symbols] which are remarkably beautiful . . . Even if the meaning of many of the signs is almost forgotten, nevertheless there is a depth of feeling in their design, and in them we see with what a wealth of emotional ideas our ancestors connected these things."

IRON VITRIOL AND AQUAFORTIS

The sign of aquafortis, resembling an interlaced cross, is worked in medium gray; the sign of iron vitriol is worked in black. Uneven diagonal stripes of three shades of bright salmon form the background.

Actual size: 11⅛″ x 8¼″

English Provincial Silver Marks

According to G. Bernard Hughes in his article "Hall-Marks on British Provincial Silver," published in *Country Life*, April 9, 1959, provincial English silver had much the same system of marks, or punches, as London silver. The earliest of these distinguishing marks, or punches, he writes, "consisted largely of symbols and emblems such as hung outside the old shops, but by the 17th century it had become more customary for the smith to use the initials of his Christian name and surname."

As early as 1300 assaying was practiced in England, and Edward I ordered that silver be of "Esterling Allay," tested on a touchstone. Our designation of silver as "sterling" is derived from the German tribe called the Easterlings, who were famous for the purity of their silver coinage.

NEWCASTLE SILVER MARK, 1672

The three turreted castles and shield are worked in three shades of gray against
a patterned background of my own devising of two tones of bright blue.

Actual size: 8″ x 8⅞″

EXETER SILVER MARK, 1715

The central motif of three turreted castles on a shield is worked in four tones of gray against a background of my own devising executed in three tones of purple.

Actual size: 7⅞″ x 10⅛″

Alphabets

The first stage of writing was pictographic, consisting of drawings of natural objects and disconnected, fragmentary pictures. Then came the ideographic stage, consisting of a fixed, pictorial symbol of an object or action. And last came the phonetic syllabic signs and symbols representing primary oral sounds. These are the basic definitions of alphabets from Tommy Thompson's *A.B.C. of our Alphabet*.

In 1912 Sir William Flinders Petrie published his book *The Formation of the Alphabet*. He firmly supported his theory that long before the ancient Mediterranean languages existed—indeed, from the beginning of the prehistoric ages—"a totally different system of linear signs, full of variety and distinction" was commonly used for commercial purposes.

But there are many conflicting theories about the origins of alphabets. Some scholars believe that our alphabet was derived from the Greek, and the Greek from the Semitic, offering as proof the Moabite stone, which bears an inscription of Mesh, King of Moab, dating from the ninth century before Christ. On the other hand, François Lenormant, famous French professor of archeology, produced his documented case, in 1874, that Egypt was the primary source of our alphabet. Still other learned men traced the beginnings to the Babylonian cuneiform, the Cyprian syllabary, or the Minoan writing of Crete. In support of this last theory, Sir Arthur Evans in *Scripta Minoa* states that the alphabet started in Crete and was transported to Palestine by the Philistines, and in turn borrowed from them by the Phoenicians.

May happy curiosity bring you to your own conclusions!

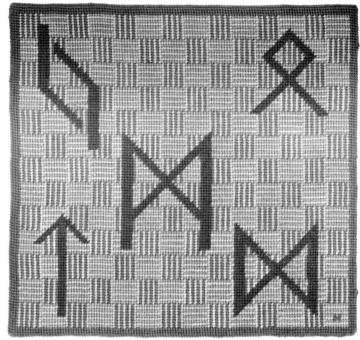

RUNES

Five Nordic runes (*upper left to bottom right*): Jara—Year; Ogal—Possession; Man—Mankind; Tir—Honor; Day—Day.

The Norwegian C. J. S. Marstrander stated in his treatise of 1928 that the runes were derived from a Northern Etruscan alphabet which was in use at the beginning of our (Christian) era in the region of the eastern Alps among Celtic tribes.

The symbols are worked in dark brown against a background of alternate squares of henna and light moss green, and light moss green and medium moss green. The border is of darker moss green.

Actual size: 13½″ x 12¼″

PART OF THE CORINTHIAN ALPHABET DERIVED FROM THE MOABITE STONE

The symbols are executed in dark brown against a marbleized background of four shades of forest green.

Actual size: 5⅛″ x 19″

106

Animals and Birds

There are three subjects that have an unspoken, unwritten language of affection—children, animals and birds, and gardens. There are no adjectives for the joy they give, and their symbolism is universal and timeless.

The animals and birds in this book are translated into needlepoint from fragments of amphorae, and I have tried to use the border patterns from backgrounds of the same period.

GREEK BIRDS

700 B.C.

The heads and bodies of the birds are worked in light henna and dark brown, and the background is of sand color and three shades of brown.

Actual size: 13″ x 8½″

OPPOSITE:

GREEK HORSE WITH BIRDS

700 B.C.

The design is worked in four shades of brown.

Actual size: 8¾″ x 6¾″

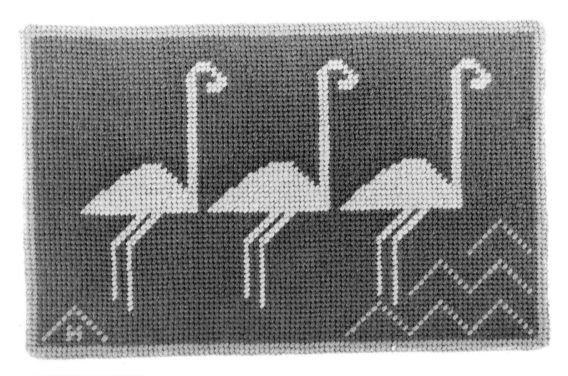

EGYPTIAN BIRDS

5000 B.C.

The birds are worked in pale buff color against a background of two shades of gray-blue.

Actual size: 11″ x 6½″

THREE EGYPTIAN DEER

5000 B.C.

The deer are worked in dark brown, with a horizontally striped background in shades of gold-brown.

Actual size: 14⅝″ x 7⅝″

Electronic Signs

As symbols reflect a period of time, these startling electronic signs have become part of a new language in the twentieth century that reveals the miracle of modern communication and heralds the future.

LOOP

The design is worked in three shades of gray.

Actual size: 9″ x 7″

ANTENNA, GROUND, CAPACITATOR

The symbols are worked in beige, the background in two shades of blue.

Actual size: 18⅛″ x 8½″

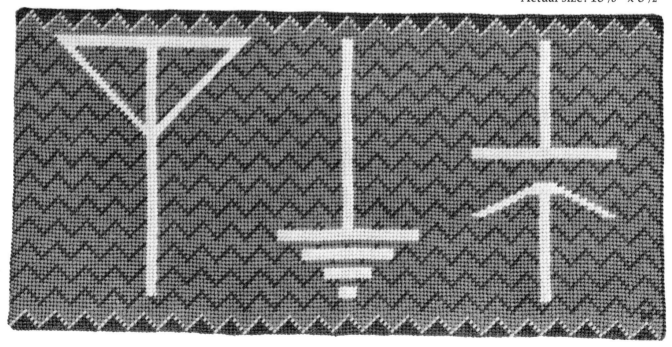

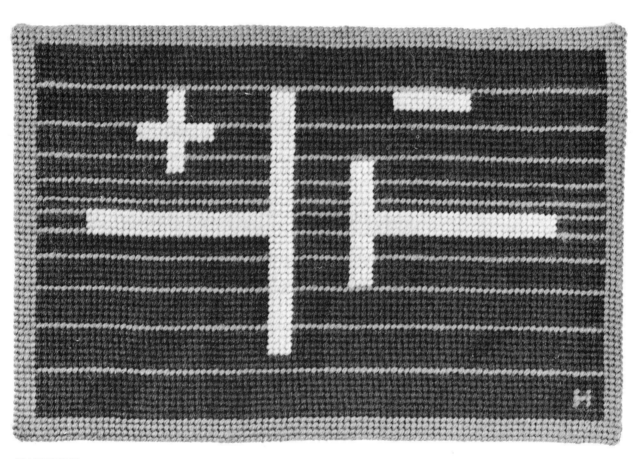

BATTERY

The symbols and background are worked in three shades of gray.

Actual size: 10⅜″ x 7¾″

Backgrounds and Borders

Because they are inherently serious and dramatic statements, the subjects in this book are intended for display and not as rug or pillow designs. As you learn to think in needlepoint, the subjects that you find in your own personal search for designs may be more appropriate for practical uses, just as my works seem most fitting for display. However, many of the repeated patterns that have been used as backgrounds and borders in this book are indeed suited for rug designs if worked on larger-mesh canvas with rug yarn. It is simply a matter of counting the stitches that make up one repeat and working them again and again to fill your canvas.

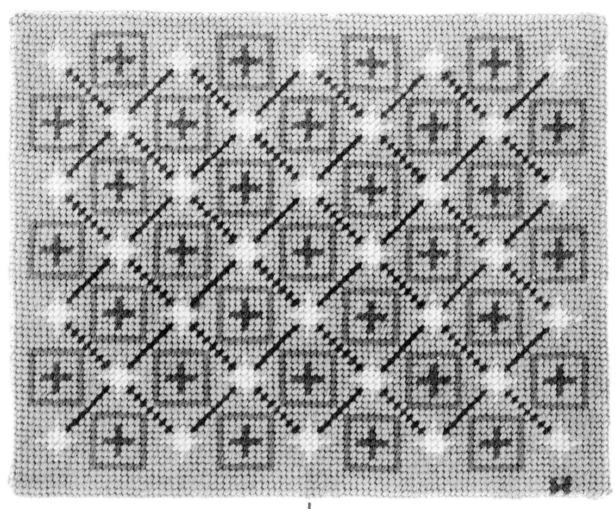

BACKGROUND

This over-all design could be used for a scatter rug, or a single band could be taken for a border. The base color is light gray-blue, the squares are a shade darker, the crosses are a light medium blue, and the lines are dark blue. The stars at the intersections of the lines seem to glitter, for they are worked in light yellow.

Actual size: 9¾″ x 7⅝″

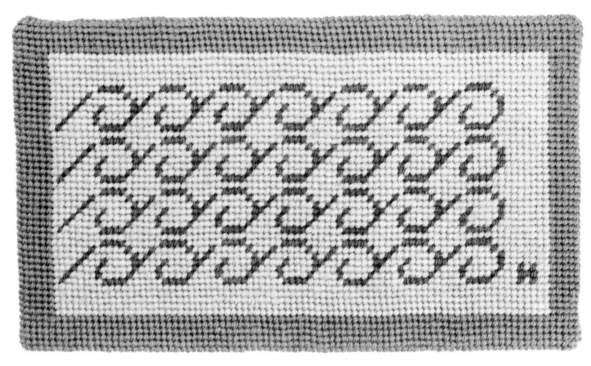

BACKGROUND

This design could also be used in various scales for a scatter rug, or in a single strip as a border.

Actual size: 8⅝″ x 4⅞″

BACKGROUND

This design can also be used for a scatter rug. It is worked in two shades of light yellow against a dark brown background.

Actual size: 8⅞″ x 6⅛″

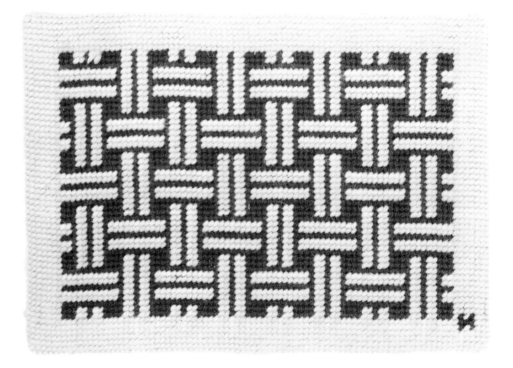

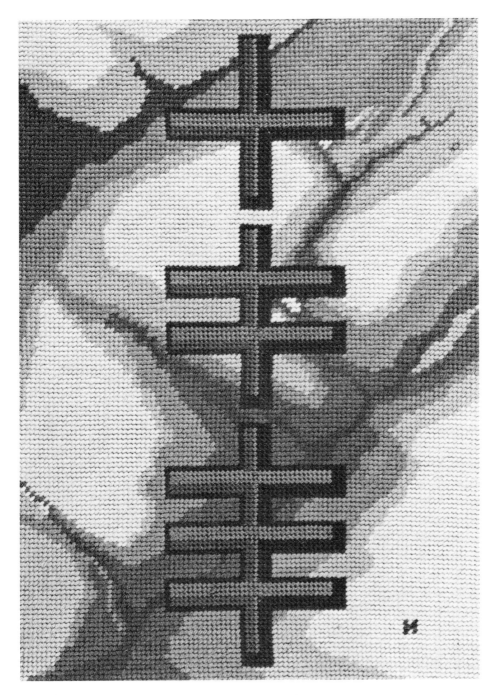

BACKGROUND

Here are three ancient botanical signs. From the top, they signify "dangerous," "pernicious," "deadly." They are worked in shades of green against a marbleized background of the same color and shades.

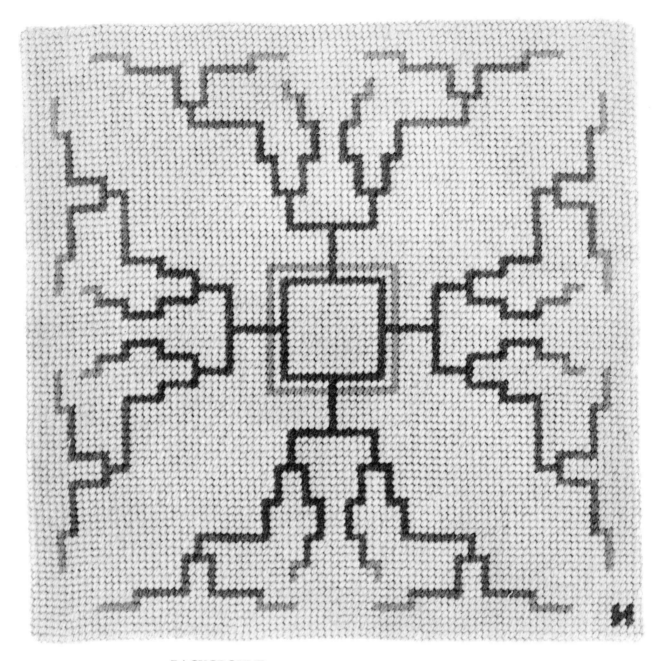

BACKGROUND

This design is worked in four shades of gray-green, and in the center square a motif could be introduced in a contrasting color.

Actual size: 9¼″ x 9″

BACKGROUND

This design is also appropriate for scatter rugs. Single strips can be used for borders. It is worked in alternate pale gold and medium gold strips, with the motifs executed in deep red.

Actual size: 8⅝″ x 10⅜″

BACKGROUND

This design can also be used in strips as a border, and in an over-all pattern for a scatter rug. Here, it is worked in dark brown on a yellow background.

Actual size: 6⅝″ x 6½″

OPPOSITE:

BACKGROUND

These are two ancient botanical signs: the top, the symbol of "tree," the single-barred motif the symbol of "shrub." Both motifs are worked in dark green, and the checked, or diapered, background is executed in two shades of pale green.

Actual size: 9⅞″ x 17⅜″

APPENDIXES

Basic Techniques

There are many books that describe needlepoint techniques, and although this book is strictly a presentation of design possibilities on canvas, it may be helpful to add a few words here about skills.

There are several diagonal stitches that result in the same bold, geometric slant recommended for executing the designs in this book, although each stitch is worked differently on the canvas.

Continental stitch: This is the only stitch I use. A most maneuverable stitch, it can be worked either from right to left or from top to bottom, and in outlining the central motif on the canvas. Do not pull the yarn too tightly as you work. When you work the stitch horizontally you can turn the canvas for each row if it is more comfortable to work consistently in one direction.

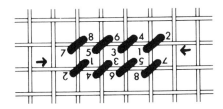

1. Starting at the right, bring the needle up from behind at (1) and pull the thread through, leaving ample thread end at the back to work into the finished design. Place stitches in the canvas as indicated by the number sequence and turn the work, if you wish, for the second row.

Half-Cross stitch: This can be used only on the penelope canvas, since the double-thread intersections of the weave are necessary for anchoring the stitch. The half-cross stitch is usually worked from left to right, even if you are left-handed.

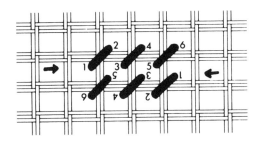

2. Follow the number sequence from left to right for the top row; turn the work, if you wish, and repeat the sequence for the second row.

The half-cross stitch can be combined with the continental stitch, and then becomes quickpoint, a most useful technique when worked on larger-meshed canvas (when there are at least five squares per inch) in rug making. In quickpoint, one row of continental is worked from right to left, and the next row, above or below the first, is worked in half-cross stitch from left to right. The canvas need not be turned to work quickpoint.

Basketweave stitch: This is the diagonal stitch that is least apt to pull the canvas out of shape and is most suitable for filling in large areas of color. Stitches are worked on the diagonal, as pictured. It takes concentration to master, but the technique is well worth learning.

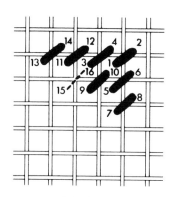

4. *The execution of the basketweave pattern. To work a diagonal line of stitches* down *from the top edge of the section, the needle passes vertically down on the back of the canvas (from 14 to 15), skipping one whole mesh.*

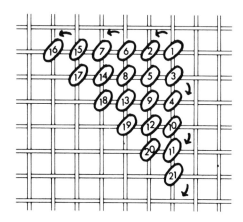

3. *Here, the numbers show the placement of whole stitches that form the basketweave pattern. Each arrow indicates the transition from the end of one diagonal row to the beginning of the next. Each stitch is always done from the bottom to the top.*

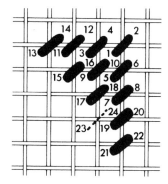

5. *To work stitches* upward *on the diagonal, from the bottom edge of the section, pass the needle horizontally across (from 22 to 23), skipping one mesh.*

To calculate how much yarn you will need for a needlepoint design you must first decide in inches how much of each color will be used to fill the canvas. For multicolored areas, be generous in estimating how much yarn of each color will be needed.

Obviously, the larger the canvas mesh, the thicker the yarn must be to cover it. You may already have a favorite combination of yarn and canvas, but if in doubt, you would be wise to seek guidance from a yarn supplier or craft store. Many department stores now feature a needlepoint counter, where you can get advice from experts. In doing needlepoint you can use a wide variety of yarns, including tapestry wool, knitting worsted, and French or Persian yarn, doubling or tripling strands when working on canvas with less than ten or twelve squares per inch.

To cover one square inch of canvas in the continental stitch you will need 36 inches of yarn for #10 mono canvas; 36 inches on 10# penelope; 42 inches on #12 mono; and 20 inches of yarn on #5 penelope.

To cover one square inch of canvas in the half-cross stitch you will need 28 inches of yarn on #10 penelope and 14 inches of yarn on #5 penelope. (The half-cross stitch is not recommended for mono canvas.)

To cover one square inch of canvas in basketweave you will need 36 inches of yarn for both #10 mono canvas and #10 penelope; 42 inches on #12 penelope; and 18 inches of yarn on #5 penelope.

Source Books

CHINESE SYMBOLS

I Ching (Book of Changes). James Legge, trans., Ch'u Chai with Winberg Chai, eds. New York, University Books, 1964.

Li Chi (Book of Rites). James Legge, trans., Ch'u Chai with Winberg Chai, eds., New York, University Books, 1967.

TIBETAN SYMBOLS

The Dalai Lama of Tibet, His Holiness. *My Land and My People.* New York, McGraw-Hill, 1962.

Norbu, Thubten Jigme. *Tibet Is My Country.* New York, E. P. Dutton, 1961.

——— and Colin M. Turnbull. *Tibet.* New York, Simon and Schuster, 1968.

Richardson, H. E. *A Short History of Tibet.* New York, E. P. Dutton, 1962.

Teachings of Tibetan Yoga. Garma C. C. Chang, trans. and annotator. New York, University Books, 1963.

Waddell, L. Austine. *Lhasa and Its Mysteries.* New York, E. P. Dutton, 1906.

Of great importance are the four catalogues of the collections of the Newark Museum, written by Eleanor Olsen, former Curator of Far Eastern Art at the museum, and published by the Newark Museum.

NEAR EAST SYMBOLS

Gothein, Marie Luise. *A History of Garden Art.* Mrs. Archer-Hind, trans., Walter P. Wright, ed. London, J. M. Dent & Sons, 1928.

Inman, Thomas. *Ancient Pagan and Modern Christian Symbolism.* Ludgate Hill, London, Trubner & Co., 1875.

CHRISTIAN SYMBOLS

Allen, J. Romilly. *Early Christian Symbolism.* Sardinia Street, London, Whiting & Co., 1887.

Coulton, G. G. *Mediaeval Faith and Symbolism.* New York, Harper & Bros., 1958.

Ferguson, George. *Signs and Symbols of Christian Art.* New York, Oxford University Press, 1954.

Hornung, Clarence P. *Designs and Devices.* New York, Dover Publications, 1946.

Koch, Rudolph. *The Book of Signs.* Vyvyan Holland, trans. Dover Publications, 1930 (paperback reprint); first published by the First Edition Club of London, 1930.

Twining, Louisa. *Symbols and Emblems of Early and Mediaeval Christian Art.* London, Longman, Brown, Green & Longman, 1852.

Webber, F. R. *Church Symbolism.* With an introduction by Ralph Adams Cram. Cleveland, J. H. Hansen, 1938.

AMERICAN INDIAN SYMBOLS

Wilson, Thomas. *The Swastika.* U.S. Printing Office, Washington, D.C., 1896.

MEXICAN FLAT AND CYLINDRICAL STAMPS

Enciso, Jorge. *Design Motifs of Ancient Mexico.* New York, Dover Publications, 1947.

HOBO SIGNS

Botkin, B. A., and Alvin F. Harlow, eds. *A Treasury of Railroad Folklore.* New York, Crown Publishers, 1953.

Lehner, Ernest. *Symbols, Signs and Signets.* New York, World Publishing, 1950.

STONEMASONS' MARKS

Coulton, G. G. *Mediaeval Faith and Symbolism.* New York, Harper Torchbooks, 1958.

Gould's History of Freemasonry Throughout the World. New York, Charles Scribner's Sons, 1936.

Koch, Rudolph. *The Book of Signs.* (See under "Christian Symbols," above.)

HOUSE MARKS AND HOLDING MARKS

Koch, Rudolph. *The Book of Signs.* (See under "Christian Symbols," above.)

MERCHANTS' MARKS, OCCUPATIONAL MARKS, AND COUNTER MARKS

Koch, Rudolph. *The Book of Signs.* (See under "Christian Symbols," above.)

HERALDIC BEASTS

Bromley, John, and Heather Child. *The Armorial Bearings of the Guilds of London.* With a foreword by Anthony R. Wagner. London, Warne & Co., 1960.

Brooke-Little, J. P. *The Colour of Heraldry.* London, published by Heraldry Society, 1958.

Elvin, Charles Norton. *A Dictionary of Heraldry.* Published by *Heraldry Today,* 10 Beauchamp Place, London, 1969.

———— *Hand-Book of Mottoes.* Published by *Heraldry Today,* 10 Beauchamp Place, London, 1963.

Lower, M. A. *The Curiosities of Heraldry.* London, John Smith, 1845.

Messenger, A. W. B. *The Heraldry of Canterbury Cathedral.* Published by office of the Friends of Christ Church Gateway, Canterbury, 1947.

Moule, Thomas. *Heraldry of Fish.* London, John Van Voorst, 1842.

Robson, Thomas. *The History of Heraldry.* Privately printed for the author by Turner & Marwood, Sunderland, Eng., 1840.

Rosenberg, Melrich V. *The Ark of Heraldry.* New York, Henry Holt, 1939.

Rothery, Guy Cadogan. *A.B.C. of Heraldry.* Philadelphia, George W. Jacobs & Co.

Scott-Giles, C. W. *Boutell's Heraldry.* London, Frederick Warne & Co., 1950.

Wagner, Anthony R. *Historic Heraldry of Britain.* London, Oxford University Press, 1939.

ARMORERS' MARKS

Lehner, Ernest. *Symbols, Signs and Signets.* New York, World Publishing, 1950.

Stone, George Cameron. *A Glossary of the Construction, Decoration and Use of Arms and Armor.* New York, Jack Bussell, 1961 (reissue).

MAGIC SIGNS

Balliet, Mrs. L. Dow. *The Philosophy of Numbers.* New York, George Sully & Co., 1927.

Budge, E. A. Wallis. *Amulets and Talismans.* New York, University Books, 1961.

Butler, E. M. *Ritual Magic.* New York, Cambridge University Press, 1949.

Givry, Grillot de. *Witchcraft, Magic and Alchemy.* J. Courtenay Locke, trans. London, George G. Harrap & Co., 1931.

Levi, Eliphas. *Transcendental Magic.* Arthur E. Waite, trans. London, William Rider & Son, 1923.

Montrose (Charles William Dunlop Adams). *Numerology for Everybody.* New York, Blue Ribbon Books, 1940.

Sepharial (Walter Gorn Old). *The Kabala of Numbers.* Philadelphia, David McKay, 1913.

Singer, Charles. *From Magic to Science.* New York, Boni & Liveright, 1928.

Spence, Lewis. *The Encyclopedia of Occultism.* New York, University Books, 1960.

Thomas, William, and Kate Pavitt. *The Book of Talismans, Amulets and Zodiacal Gems.* London, Rider & Co., 1914.

Thorndike, Lynn. *The History of Magic and Experimental Science During the First Thirteen Centuries of Our Era.* New York, Macmillan, 1929.

Waite, Arthur E. *The Book of Ceremonial Magic.* New York, University Books, 1961.

ASTROLOGICAL SIGNS

Budge, E. A. Wallis. *Amulets and Talismans.* New York, University Books (republished) 1961.

Hammond, Natalie Hays. *Anthology of Pattern.* With an introduction by George Boas. William Helburn, 1949.

Koch, Rudolph. *The Book of Signs.* (See under "Christian Symbols," above.)

ANCIENT CHEMICAL SIGNS

Koch, Rudolph. *The Book of Signs.* (See under "Christian Symbols," above.)

ENGLISH PROVINCIAL SILVER MARKS

Bigelow, Francis Hill. *Historic Silver of the Colonies and Its Makers.* Macmillan, 1917.

ALPHABETS

Hammond, Natalie Hays. *Anthology of Pattern.* (See under "Astrological Signs," above.)

Thompson, Tommy. *A.B.C. of Our Alphabet.* New York, Studio Publications, 1942.

Tymms, W. R. *The Art of Illuminating as Practiced in Europe from the Earliest Times.* With an essay and instructions by Archbishop M. D. Wyatt. London, Day & Son, n.d.